101 VEGETARIAN GRILL & BBQ RECIPES

AUBERGINE/EGGPLANT with honey & spices
PAGE 40

101
VEGETARIAN
GRILL & BBQ
RECIPES

AMAZING MEAT-FREE RECIPES FOR
VEGETARIAN & VEGAN BBQ FOOD

rps

RYLAND PETERS & SMALL
LONDON • NEW YORK

First published in the UK in 2016
by Ryland Peters & Small
20–21 Jockey's Fields
London WC1R 4BW
and
341 E 116th St
New York, NY 10029

www.rylandpeters.com

Recipe collection compiled
by Alice Sambrook
Recipe text © Amy Ruth Finegold,
Annie Rigg, Brian Glover, Carol
Hilker, Celia Brooks Brown, Chloe
Coker, Claire and Lucy McDonald,
Dunja Gulin, Fran Warde, Ghillie
Basan, Jackie Kearney, Jane
Montgomery, Jane Noraika, Jordan
Bourke, Laura Washburn, Lesley
Waters, Lindy Wildsmith, Louise
Pickford, Lydia France, Miranda
Ballard, Tori Finch, Tori Haschka,
Valerie Aikman-Smith

Design & photography
© Ryland Peters & Small 2016

A CIP catalog record for this
is available from the Library
Congress and the British Lib

ISBN: 978-1-84975-722-5

Printed in China

10 9 8 7 6 5 4 3 2 1

Editor: Alice Sambrook
Designer: Paul Stradling
Production: David Hearn
Editorial Director: Julia Charles
Art Director: Leslie Harrington
Publisher: Cindy Richards
Indexer: Vanessa Bird

NOTES

• See page 9 for guidance on vegetarian cheeses.

• All eggs are medium (UK) or large (US), unless otherwise specified. It is recommended that free-range, organic eggs be used whenever possible. Recipes containing raw or partially cooked egg should not be served to the very young, very old, anyone with a compromised immune system or pregnant women.

• When a recipe calls for grated zest of citrus fruit, buy unwaxed fruit and wash well before use. If you can only find treated fruit, scrub and rinse before using.

• Ovens should be preheated to the specified temperatures. All ovens work slightly differently.

CONTENTS

INTRODUCTION

IS THERE ANY FORM OF COOKING MORE SATISFYING THAN GRILLING OVER A PIT OF RED-HOT GLOWING COALS? ENVELOPED IN HEAT AND SLOWLY-DRIFTING-CLOUDS OF SWEET-SMELLING SMOKE; A TANG OF CITRUS JUICE, A WAFT OF FRAGRANT HERBS, THE AROMA OF EARTHY SPICES FROM YOUR PERFECTLY PREPARED MARINADE, AND – WAIT FOR IT – NOT A MEATY SAUSAGE IN SIGHT! GALVANIZE YOUR GRILL AND GET READY TO BARBECUE, VEGETARIAN STYLE.

For many, cooking on a barbecue is a real labour of love, working away to deliver platters of beautifully smoky and chargrilled food to willing hands. But its not quite what you'd call 'hard' work. Standing in the sunshine with a glass of your favourite ice-cold beverage, chatting and cooking as the mood takes you. If your attention wanders for a minute, the charred bits are the good bits! And there is nothing like a barbecue/grill party to bring people together – an improbable mix of mums, dads, aunties, uncles, cheeky children, and friends, chatting, joking, and eating together. A dining event and an easy-going sense of occasion that many of us seem to have lost in our busy everyday lives. The pleasure of al fresco dining is one normally reserved for holidays or vacations, but barbecues give us a chance to enjoy cooking and eating outside whatever the weather. Be it a light kebab and salad for a scorching summer day or ember-roasted hot potatoes, hearty burgers and toasted s'mores for those chilly, cosy festive cookouts.

What's more, there is no need to be sidelined by overbearing carnivores. You will never run out of steam with 101 tasty vegetarian recipes to try, ranging from fresh and simple to deliciously gourmet. No one will miss the meat sweats when you serve up dish after dish as good as this. Vegetables were just born to be rubbed with spice mix or enveloped in marinade and sizzled on a hot grill. Gone are the days of a sad 1 option menu, a whole range of meat-free delights awaits.

GRILLING GUIDELINES

CHOOSING A BARBECUE/GRILL
Outdoor barbecues/grills come in all shapes, sizes, varieties and prices – from the small disposable foil ones sold in supermarkets or hardware stores, to larger and often hugely expensive options. Some have both a rack and a flat plate, for versatility, but this is not essential. The recipes will work on any of the following.

Purists may argue that charcoal has to fuel a barbecue/grill, but many people prefer (and find it easier to opt for) gas or electric ones. It is certainly debatable as to what will give the best flavour to the food, but it really comes down to personal choice.

For a charcoal barbecue/grill, you can use either standard briquettes or hardwood lump charcoal. The former may contain chemicals from the process used to make them, which – although totally safe – may affect the flavour of the food. Hardwood lump charcoal is not as readily available as briquettes, but contains no additives, burns easily, gets far hotter and lasts longer.

Portable barbecues/grills are essential if you want to cook away from home (unless your chosen site has permanent grills), and these too come in a wide selection of styles. Be aware of weight, since someone has to carry it – the lighter the better. Portable barbecues/grills can also be either charcoal- or gas-fired, but remember that coals stay hot for some time, so you must find somewhere you can legally and safely leave them or wait until they are completely cool before packing them in a bag to take away with you.

A ridged grill pan/griddle pan on the stovetop is an option if the weather is really bad or you don't have much space on the barbecue outside. Good for getting those chargrilled lines but you won't get so much of that classic smoky flavour.

Safety is extremely important in barbecuing, especially if you are in a public park. Be sensible and set the barbecue up away from dry timber or grass. Take a fire blanket or, if possible, a small portable fire extinguisher.

COOKING ON A CHARCOAL GRILL

Arrange the fuel in as large an area as your barbecue/grill will allow, at least 10 cm/4 inches deep and leaving a little room around the edges. Place a few firelighters among the coals and light them using a taper or matches – they will help to get the fire started. Once the coals are burning, leave them for 40–45 minutes, until all the flames have subsided and the coals are covered in grey ash. Hold your hand about 12 cm/5 inches above the fire and count how long it can stay there. It will be only a couple seconds for a hot fire; 3–4 seconds for medium heat; and 5–6 seconds for a cool fire.

You can also determine the temperature for cooking by adjusting the height of the grill rack over the coals. Most charcoal grills have several rungs to set the wire rack on, the closest to the heat being the hottest and the farthest away the coolest. Cleaning is best done after you have finished cooking but while the barbecue/grill is still assembled, so that any residual bits of food can be brushed off into the fire. Do not clean the rack with soap or water, just scrub it well with a sturdy wire brush (see equipment, right).

GAS OR ELECTRIC?

Gas and electric barbecues/grills can be adjusted in the same way as a domestic stove, by turning the temperature up or down. They often come with a hood, enabling you to cover the food as it cooks, which produces a similar effect to roasting. Alternatively, leave the lid off and grill as normal.

It is important to preheat a gas or electric barbecue/grill until it is really hot before adding the food, and then reduce the heat as necessary. This enables the food to brown quickly on the outside, sealing in the flavour, in the same way as on a traditional charcoal barbecue/grill.

Cleaning is also done in the same way as for the charcoal barbecue/grill, although you can buy special cleaners from hardware stores. For best results, follow the instructions on the back of individual products.

EQUIPMENT

Long-handled tongs are essential for turning over fiddly bits of food without allowing your hands to get too close to the heat and scorching.

Choose a sturdy **spatula** with a wide head that can support the weight of heavier burgers. A heatproof silicone head is also useful and cleans easily.

Skewers can be either bamboo or metal. Bamboo skewers are disposable and will need to be soaked before use, to prevent them from burning over a high heat. Metal skewers are readily available from hardware stores, but remember they can get very hot, so turn them using a kitchen cloth or tongs.

A barbecue basting brush is essential for topping up food with glazes and marinades as it cooks.

A sturdy wire brush is the best tool for cleaning and removing bits of stuck-on food from the surface of the grill or flat plate.

FOOD PREPARATION

Get all the food preparation done in advance – the day, the morning or an hour or two before you eat. Marinating times in the recipes are flexible, so do what suits you.

Salsas, relishes, dressings and salads can be made in advance, but green salads should be dressed at the last minute. Once prepared, cover the food and refrigerate or store it in a cool place until you are ready to cook or serve it. Always keep food covered with clingfilm/plastic wrap or a clean kitchen cloth while it is waiting to be cooked, to keep off the bugs. Food should then be cooked as quickly as possible to prevent it from spoiling. Keep a warm oven or warming rack on stand-by to keep dishes hot if you are cooking in batches. Keep hungry guests happy in the meantime with snacks and small plates or sharing platters that can be laid out in advance. Make sure you have any dips, relishes or sauces ready for people to help themselves when the main event arrives.

A note on vegetarian cheese

Cheeses started with animal rennet are not suitable for strict vegetarians so read food labelling carefully and, if necessary, check that the cheese you buy is made with a non-animal (microbial) starter. Traditional Parmesan is not vegetarian, instead you could use vegetarian hard cheese (such as Gran Moravia which has the same texture so is ideal for grating) or Parma (a vegan product). There is an increasing number of manufacturers who are now producing vegetarian or vegan versions of traditionally non-vegetarian cheeses, such as Gruyère or Gorgonzola. Check online for suppliers and stockists in your location. Always check the label carefully first before using any products.

CHAPTER 1
DIPS, SMALL BITES & APPETIZERS

SWEET POTATO HUMMUS

1 large sweet potato, baked until very tender, flesh scooped

400-g/14-oz. can chickpeas (a few reserved for the garnish)

2 garlic cloves, peeled

6 tablespoons tahini

½ teaspoon each cumin and coriander seeds, gently toasted in a dry pan until fragrant

grated zest and juice of ½ lemon

3–4 tablespoons extra virgin olive oil

1 teaspoon sea salt

1 tablespoon freshly chopped parsley, to garnish

serves 8

★ Put the cooked potato flesh, chickpeas, garlic and tahini in a food processor and blitz together. Using a pestle and mortar, grind the cumin and coriander seeds to a powder and add to the processor (reserving a pinch to garnish). Add the lemon zest and juice, salt and 3 tablespoons olive oil. Blitz again until you have a soft, smooth purée, adding more olive oil if the mixture is stiff. Season to taste.

★ Serve drizzled with olive oil, and sprinkled with reserved chickpeas, spices and parsley to garnish.

BABA GHANOUSH

2 aubergines/eggplants

2 garlic cloves, peeled

4 tablespoons tahini

3 tablespoons freshly squeezed lemon juice

½ teaspoon sea salt

a generous pinch of sweet paprika

2 tablespoons extra virgin olive oil

1 tablespoon pomegranate seeds

serves 8

★ Light your gas hob/burner on the lowest setting. Pierce the flesh of the aubergines/eggplants once or twice and place directly onto the flame. Char the skin all over, turning now and again until the flesh is soft and the skin blistered. Allow to cool completely. Carefully peel away the skin, keeping any juice that comes out.

★ Put aubergine/eggplant flesh, garlic, tahini, lemon juice, salt, paprika and olive oil in a food processor. Blitz until smooth and then season generously.

★ Serve drizzled with olive oil and sprinkled with pomegranate seeds.

BORLOTTI BEAN PURÉE

250 g/1⅔ cups fresh borlotti beans

400 ml/1⅔ cups extra virgin olive oil

2 tablespoons red wine vinegar

5 garlic cloves, peeled

1 tablespoon freshly chopped rosemary leaves (stalks removed)

a handful of baby plum tomatoes

sea salt

serves 8

★ Place the beans in a large ovenproof pot of water. Bring almost to the boil, then cover and reduce to a gentle simmer for 1 hour or until just tender.

★ Preheat the oven to 200°C (400°F) Gas 6.

★ Drain, leaving about 100 ml/ ½ cup water at the bottom, add the olive oil, vinegar, garlic, rosemary, tomatoes and 1 teaspoon salt. Bake in the preheated oven for 30 minutes or until the beans have become soft. Remove from the oven and allow to cool. Bash everything with a potato masher. Season to taste and serve.

cornbread muffins

480 ml/2 cups milk

2 eggs

110 g/1 stick butter, melted

375 g/3 cups plain/all-purpose flour

225 g/1½ cups cornmeal

1 teaspoon salt

4 teaspoons baking powder

110 g/½ cup plus 1 tablespoon sugar

198-g/7-oz. can (sweet)corn kernels, drained (or use fresh corn kernels cut straight from 2 cobs/ears of corn)

a 6-hole muffin pan, lined with paper muffin cases

mango guacamole

3 large ripe avocados

½ small red onion, finely chopped

1 red chilli/chile, deseeded and finely chopped

freshly squeezed juice of 1 lime

1 ripe mango, peeled, pitted and chopped into chunks

1 tablespoon freshly chopped coriander/cilantro

sea salt

serves 6

CORNBREAD MUFFINS
with mango guacamole

CORNBREAD IS ONE OF THOSE COMFORT FOODS THAT GETS EVERYONE SMILING. THIS RECIPE SEES THE CORNBREAD BAKED AS SAVOURY MUFFINS, ALTHOUGH YOU COULD ALSO COOK IT IN A CAST IRON PAN/SKILLET OVER A BARBECUE OR GRILL. GREAT SERVED WITH THE GUACAMOLE OR SLATHERED IN BUTTER OR MELTED MONTEREY JACK.

★ Preheat the oven to 220°C (425°F) Gas 7.

★ In a large mixing bowl, whisk together the milk, eggs and melted butter. In a separate large bowl, combine the flour, cornmeal, salt, baking powder and sugar. Make a well in the centre and slowly pour in the milk mixture, a little at a time, stirring until you have the consistency of a cake batter. Do not overmix otherwise the cornbread could come out a little tough. Lastly, stir through the (sweet)corn kernels.

★ Pour the dough mixture into the prepared muffin pan just to the top. Bake in the top of the preheated oven for about 20–25 minutes, until the cornbread is a deep golden colour and springy to touch.

★ To make the mango guacamole: cut the avocado in half lengthways, slicing around the pit. Holding one half of the avocado in each hand, twist your hands in opposite directions to open up the avocado. Dislodge the pit and discard it, then scoop the avocado flesh out into a mixing bowl and mash it with a fork. Add the onion, chilli/chile and lime juice and mix well. Season with a pinch of salt, mix again and then gently stir in three quarters of the chopped mango and most of the chopped coriander/cilantro.

★ To serve, transfer the guacamole to a serving bowl and garnish with the remaining mango and the reserved sprinkling of chopped herbs.

Ingredients

1 head radicchio Treviso, quartered

1 head Romaine/cos lettuce, quartered

2 small fennel bulbs, with fronds, quartered

6 courgettes/zucchini halved

160 g/5 oz. cherry tomatoes

6 aubergines/eggplants, halved

extra virgin olive oil, to drizzle

a handful of freshly torn flat-leaf parsley, to garnish

marinade

75 ml/½ cup extra virgin olive oil

60 ml/¼ cup Spanish sherry vinegar

2 garlic cloves, finely chopped

1 shallot, finely chopped

a pinch of Spanish smoked paprika (pimentón)

sea salt and cracked black pepper

herbed toasts

115 g/1 stick unsalted butter, at room temperature

2 tablespoons fresh oregano leaves

2 tablespoons fresh marjoram leaves

2 tablespoons fresh thyme leaves

1 tablespoon fresh rosemary leaves

sea salt and cracked black pepper

1 large baguette, thickly sliced

serves 6–8

GRILLED MARKET VEGETABLE SALAD with herbed toasts

THIS RECIPE IS JUST RIPE FOR A VISIT TO THE FARMERS' MARKET, WHEN YOU COME HOME LADEN WITH A KALEIDOSCOPE OF COLOURFUL VEGETABLES. FOLLOW THE SUGGESTIONS BELOW OR MAKE UP YOUR OWN CHOICE. IT CAN BE A COMBINATION OF ANYTHING FROM TOMATOES TO SQUASH TO CELERY. PILE THE BEAUTIFULLY CHARRED VEGETABLES ONTO A LARGE WOODEN BOARD WITH GRILLED TOASTS AND SERVE. SIMPLE OUTDOOR SUMMER GRILLING AND EATING AT ITS BEST.

★ Put all the vegetables in a large ceramic baking dish. Mix together the marinade ingredients and pour over the vegetables. Toss to coat well and set aside.

★ Put the butter and herbs in a food processor and blitz until smooth but leaving a little texture in the butter. Season to taste with sea salt and cracked black pepper. Spread a generous amount on both sides of the baguette slices and set aside.

★ Preheat the barbecue/grill. In batches, grill the vegetables, turning them over, until slightly charred all over. Some vegetables will cook quicker than others so remove these from the barbecue/grill as they are cooked so that they don't burn. Transfer the vegetables to a large wooden board and dress lightly with any remaining marinade.

★ Barbecue/grill the baguette slices until well toasted and place on the board alongside the vegetables. Sprinkle generously with the coarse sea salt, drizzle with olive oil, and garnish with fresh parsley, to serve.

GRILLED ARTICHOKES
with chilli/chile-lime mayonnaise

TRY TO FIND SMALL OR BABY ARTICHOKES FOR THIS DISH SO THAT THEY CAN BE COOKED UNTIL TENDER STRAIGHT ON THE BARBECUE/ GRILL WITHOUT THE NEED TO BLANCH FIRST.

★ To make the mayonnaise, cover the chipotle with boiling water and let soak for 30 minutes. Drain and pat dry, then cut in half and scrape out the seeds.

★ Finely chop the chilli/chile flesh and put in a food processor. Add the egg yolks and a little salt and blend briefly until frothy. With the blade running, gradually pour the oil through the funnel until the sauce is thick and glossy. Add the lime juice and, if the mayonnaise is too thick, 1 tablespoon warm water. Taste and adjust the seasoning with salt and pepper, if necessary, then cover and set aside.

★ Trim the stalks from the artichokes and cut off the top 2.5 cm/1 inch of the globes. Slice the globes in half lengthways, cutting out the central 'choke' if necessary. Rub the cut surfaces with lemon juice to stop them discolouring.

★ Preheat the barbecue/grill.

★ Toss the artichokes with the oil and a little salt and pepper. Cook on the preheated barbecue/grill for about 15–20 minutes, depending on size, until charred and tender, turning halfway through the cooking time. Serve with the chilli/chile-lime mayonnaise and wedges of lime.

18 small artichokes

1 lemon, cut in half

2 tablespoons extra virgin olive oil

sea salt and freshly ground black pepper

lime wedges, to serve

chilli/chile-lime mayonnaise

1 dried chipotle chilli/chile

2 egg yolks

200 ml/1⅓ cups olive oil

freshly squeezed juice of 1 lime

serves 6

GRILLED POLENTA

BARBECUED OR GRILLED POLENTA/CORNMEAL TRIANGLES MAKE A LOVELY ACCOMPANIMENT FOR MAIN DISHES OR THEY CAN BE USED AS A BRUSCHETTA-TYPE BASE FOR VEGETABLES, SUCH AS THE VEGETABLE ANTIPASTO (SEE PAGE 20).

2 teaspoons salt

175 g/1¼ cups instant polenta/cornmeal

2 garlic cloves, crushed

1 tablespoon freshly chopped basil

50 g/3½ tablespoons butter

50 g/¾ cup freshly grated Italian-style hard cheese

freshly ground black pepper

olive oil, for brushing

a rectangular cake pan, 23 x 30 cm/ 9 x 12 inches, greased

serves 8

★ Pour 1 litre/4¼ cups water into a heavy-based saucepan and bring to the boil. Add the salt and gradually beat in the polenta/cornmeal in a steady stream, using a large, metal whisk.

★ Cook over low heat, stirring constantly with a wooden spoon for 5 minutes or until the grains have swelled and thickened.

★ Remove the saucepan from the heat and immediately beat in the garlic, basil, butter and Italian-style hard cheese until the mixture is smooth. Pour into the greased pan and let cool completely.

★ Preheat the barbecue/grill.

★ Turn out the polenta/cornmeal onto a board and cut into large squares, then cut in half again to form triangles. Brush the triangles with a little olive oil and cook on the preheated barbecue/grill for 2–3 minutes on each side until charred and heated through.

TOMATO KEFTEDES with tzatziki

400 g/14 oz. ripe cherry tomatoes

½ red onion, very finely chopped

a large handful of fresh basil, chopped

a large handful of fresh mint, chopped

1 teaspoon dried oregano

a large handful of fresh flat-leaf parsley, chopped

100 g/¾ cup self-raising/self-rising flour

250 ml/1½ cups olive oil

750 ml/4½ cups sunflower or canola oil

tzatziki

1 cucumber

350 g/12 oz. Greek yogurt

2 tablespoons lemon juice

2 garlic cloves, finely chopped

1 tablespoon extra virgin olive oil

salt and freshly ground black pepper

makes 16 keftedes, enough for 4 as an appetizer

THERE ARE PLENTY OF FLAVOURS AND TEXTURES AT PLAY IN THESE GORGEOUS GREEK TOMATO FRITTERS. THEY ARE SIMPLY ONIONS AND GREEN HERBS BOUND TOGETHER WITH PINCHED TOMATO FLESH AND FLOUR, THEN FRIED UNTIL GOLDEN AND CRISP. SERVE WITH TZATZIKI, AS A DELICIOUS LITTLE NIBBLE WHILE THE BARBECUE/GRILL IS HEATING.

★ For the tomato keftedes, put the tomatoes in a large bowl and pinch them so that the juices spurt out (be careful to pinch them facing downwards, otherwise you'll end up with pulp in your eye). Keep pinching and tearing at the flesh until you're left with a pile of seeds, juices and pulp. Add the onion, basil, mint, oregano, parsley and salt and pepper to the pulp. You can use a potato masher at this point to make sure everything is well incorporated.

★ Add half the flour and stir. Add the second half slowly. You want a thick and sticky paste the texture of a thick batter.

★ Heat the oils in a deep, heavy-based pan until small bubbles form on the surface. Make sure the oil is at least 5 cm/2 inches deep. Use a greased tablespoon to drop in the batter. After 30 seconds, rotate the fritter so it doesn't stick to the bottom. Fry for another 30 seconds or until the outside is crispy and deep red. Drain well on paper towels. Fry no more than 3 at a time.

★ For the tzatziki, cut the cucumber in half lengthways and use a teaspoon to scrape out the seeds. Grate the 2 halves into a clean kitchen cloth. Gather up the edges and squeeze out as much excess liquid as you can. Whisk together the yogurt, lemon juice, garlic and olive oil. Add the cucumber flesh and stir.

★ Season the fritters with salt and serve hot with tzatziki.

VEGETABLE ANTIPASTO

SERVING A LARGE PLATTER OF GRILLED VEGETABLES
PROVIDES A LOVELY START TO ANY BARBECUE PARTY –
CHOOSE A COMBINATION OF YOUR FAVOURITES. SERVE
WITH SOME FRESH, CRUSTY BREAD.

2 red (bell) peppers

4 baby fennel bulbs

1 large aubergine/eggplant

1 red onion

2 large courgettes/zucchini

a few fresh herb leaves, such as basil, dill, fennel, mint and flat-leaf parsley

extra virgin olive oil, to taste

freshly squeezed lemon juice, to taste

sea salt and freshly ground black pepper

crusty bread, to serve

marinade

2 sprigs each rosemary and thyme

4 bay leaves

2 garlic cloves, chopped

pared zest of 1 unwaxed lemon

1 teaspoon cracked black peppercorns

250 ml/1½ cups extra virgin olive oil

serves 4

★ Cut the (bell) peppers into quarters and discard the seeds. Trim the fennel, reserving the fronds, and cut the bulbs into slim slices. Cut the aubergine/eggplant into thick slices and cut in half again. Cut the onion into wedges and the courgettes/zucchini into thick diagonal slices.

★ For the marinade, strip the rosemary and thyme leaves from their stalks and put in a mortar. Add the bay leaves, garlic and lemon zest and pound with a pestle. Put the mixture in a bowl and stir in the peppercorns and olive oil.

★ Put all the vegetables in a bowl, pour over the marinade and toss gently to evenly coat. Cover and leave in a cool place for at least 1 hour.

★ Preheat the barbecue/grill, add the vegetables, and cook until they are all tender and lightly charred. Let cool, then peel the (bell) peppers.

★ Arrange the vegetables on a large platter, sprinkle with the herbs, reserved fennel fronds, olive oil and lemon juice, then season lightly with salt and pepper. Serve at room temperature with crusty bread.

PIRI PIRI MUSHROOMS

MAKE SURE TO SERVE THESE FIERY MUSHROOMS WITH COCKTAIL STICKS/TOOTHPICKS TO ENCOURAGE GUESTS TO ONLY TAKE ONE AT A TIME, AS THEY ARE VERY HOT! FINISHING OFF COOKING ON THE BARBECUE/GRILL WILL ADD EXTRA SMOKY FLAVOUR, IF DESIRED.

piri piri

2 large red chillies/chiles

2 garlic cloves

2 teaspoons sea salt

2 teaspoons white wine vinegar

2 tablespoons olive oil

mushrooms

2 tablespoons olive oil

1 garlic clove, crushed

400 g/6 cups baby button mushrooms

a large handful of fresh flat-leaf parsley, chopped

cocktail sticks/toothpicks

makes about 30

★ Blend all the piri piri ingredients in a food processor until you have a smooth liquid.

★ For the mushrooms, gently heat the olive oil in a large saucepan, add the garlic, mushrooms and half the parsley and cook over a medium heat for 3–4 minutes. Turn up the heat, add the piri piri mixture and cook for a further 3–4 minutes, using a wooden spoon to stir the mushrooms and prevent them from sticking.

★ Scatter in the remaining parsley, stir and serve straight away in a shallow dish with cocktail sticks/toothpicks on the side for spearing (just as you would if serving olives).

★ Finish off cooking the mushrooms on the barbecue/grill for an extra smoky flavour.

350 g/4½ cups cauliflower florets

sunflower oil, for deep-frying

lime wedges, to serve

chutney

1 onion, chopped

1–2 garlic cloves, chopped

a large handful of fresh coriander/cilantro leaves

2–3 tablespoons freshly grated/shredded or desiccated coconut

1 teaspoon caster/superfine sugar

freshly squeezed juice of ½ lemon

sea salt

batter

150 g/1¼ cups gram (chickpea) flour

2 teaspoons ground turmeric

1 teaspoon ground coriander

1 teaspoon ground fenugreek

1 teaspoon cayenne pepper or chilli/chili powder

½ teaspoon bicarbonate of soda/baking soda

1–2 teaspoons cumin seeds, crushed

sea salt and freshly ground black pepper

a packet of short wooden or bamboo skewers, to serve (optional)

serves 4

CAULIFLOWER FRITTER SATAY with coriander/cilantro & coconut chutney

THESE INDIAN-STYLE CAULIFLOWER FRITTERS MAKE A TASTY SATAY SNACK. THEY ARE PERFECT SERVED WITH THE REFRESHING YET SWEET CHUTNEY, BUT FOR A QUICK OPTION SWEET SOY SAUCE OR EVEN TOMATO KETCHUP WOULD ALSO WORK.

★ First prepare the coriander/cilantro and coconut chutney. Using a pestle and mortar, or an electric blender, pound the onion with the garlic and salt. Add the coriander/cilantro leaves and mix to a paste. Beat in the coconut, sugar and lemon juice and thin with a little water to form a smooth purée. Set aside.

★ Sift the gram (chickpea) flour with the ground spices and bicarbonate of soda/baking soda into a bowl. Add the cumin seeds and seasoning and bind with enough water to form a thick batter.

★ Heat sufficient oil in a wok or large frying pan/skillet for deep-frying. Dip the cauliflower florets into the batter and drop them into the oil, working in batches, and cook until golden brown. Drain them on paper towels. Spear each cauliflower fritter with a skewer, if using, and serve hot with the coriander/cilantro and coconut chutney for dipping.

SPINACH & RICOTTA STUFFED ONIONS

STUFFED ONIONS ARE MUCH EASIER TO MAKE THAN YOU MIGHT THINK AND CAN BE PREPARED AHEAD OF TIME, SO THEY ARE IDEAL FOR ENTERTAINING. THESE ARE FILLED WITH CREAMY RICOTTA AND SPINACH, BUT THEY COULD ALSO BE FILLED WITH A NUT-BASED STUFFING. TRY SERVING THEM WITH A FRESH GREEN SALAD ON THE SIDE.

8 red or white onions

2 tablespoons olive oil

75 g/1½ cups spinach, finely chopped

250 g/9 oz. ricotta

grated zest and juice of ½ lemon

½ teaspoon grated nutmeg

pine nuts/kernels and breadcrumbs for topping

salt and freshly ground black pepper

serves 4

★ Preheat the oven to 180°C (350°F) Gas 4.

★ Cut the root off the onions so that they sit flat. Then cut about 2 cm/ ¾ inch off the tops and peel away the skins. Hollow out the inside of the onions with a teaspoon, leaving the outer 1 or 2 layers. If there is a hole in the bottom of the onion, use a piece of the onion that has been removed to fill it in.

★ Put a large sheet of kitchen foil on a baking sheet – enough to wrap the onions, and put the onions on top. Season the onions with salt and pepper, drizzle with olive oil, pour in 2 tablespoons water, then wrap to enclose the onions in foil. Bake in the preheated oven for 30 minutes or until the onions are soft.

★ To prepare the filling, wilt the spinach in a saucepan set over low heat. Drain off any excess moisture and let cool. Put the ricotta, spinach, lemon zest and juice, nutmeg and salt and pepper in a bowl and stir well.

★ Fill the baked onions with the spinach mixture and top with a handful of pine nuts/kernels and breadcrumbs to add some crunch to the tops. Put the onions on a baking sheet and return to the oven for 15 minutes or until the tops are golden. Serve immediately with a fresh green salad on the side.

AUBERGINE/EGGPLANT & CHEESE ROLLS

2 aubergines/eggplants, cut lengthways into about 5 slices

1 teaspoon chilli/chile oil

125 ml/¾ cup olive oil

3 teaspoons cumin seeds, lightly toasted in a dry frying pan/skillet and ground

2 garlic cloves, crushed

1 red chilli/chile, deseeded and finely chopped

a large handful of fresh mint leaves, finely chopped

175 g/6 oz. firm smoked cheese, sliced

sea salt and freshly ground black pepper

a large handful of fresh coriander/cilantro, coarsely chopped, to serve

freshly squeezed juice of ½ lemon, to serve

makes 10 rolls

TRULY AT HOME IN BOTH MIDDLE EASTERN AND MEDITERRANEAN CUISINES, AUBERGINES/EGGPLANTS ARE COMPATIBLE WITH ENDLESS SPICES AND HERBS. IN THIS DISH, THEY SOAK UP THE FRAGRANCE OF SPICES AND ARE PAIRED WITH SMOKED CHEESE, ENHANCING THE ALREADY SMOKY BARBECUE FLAVOUR.

★ Arrange the aubergine/eggplant slices on a large tray. Mix both oils with the cumin, garlic, chilli/chile, mint, salt and pepper in a measuring jug/pitcher, then pour over the aubergines/eggplants. Turn each slice over so that both sides are well coated. Cover with clingfilm/plastic wrap and set aside for a few hours or overnight to soak up all the flavours.

★ Preheat the barbecue/grill. Add the aubergines/eggplants and cook for about 4 minutes, then turn and cook the other side until tender and browned.

★ Remove from the heat, put some of the cheese at one end of a slice of aubergine/eggplant and roll up firmly (do this while the aubergine/eggplant is hot so the cheese melts). Repeat with the other slices. Sprinkle with the coriander/cilantro and lemon juice, then serve.

GRILLED ROSEMARY FLATBREAD

HOT FROM THE BARBECUE OR GRILL, THIS AROMATIC HERB BREAD IS DELICIOUS USED TO MOP UP ANY WONDERFUL JUICES OR EATEN ON ITS OWN WITH OLIVE OIL FOR DIPPING.

★ Sift the flour into the bowl of an electric mixer and stir in the yeast, salt and rosemary. Add the hot water and olive oil and knead with the dough hook at high speed for about 8 minutes or until the dough is smooth and elastic.

Alternatively, sift the flour into a large bowl and stir in the yeast, salt and rosemary. Make a well in the centre, then add the hot water and olive oil and mix to form a soft dough. Turn out onto a lightly floured work surface and knead until the dough is smooth and elastic.

★ Shape the dough into a ball, then put it in an oiled bowl. Cover with a kitchen cloth and let rise in a warm place for 45–60 minutes, or until doubled in size.

★ Punch down the dough and divide into quarters. Roll each piece out on a lightly floured work surface to make a 15 cm/6 inch long oval.

★ Preheat the barbecue/grill. Brush the bread with a little olive oil and cook for 5 minutes over low heat. Brush the top with the remaining olive oil, flip and cook for a further 4–5 minutes until the bread is cooked through. Serve hot.

250 g/2 cups strong white bread flour, plus extra for dusting

1½ teaspoons fast-acting yeast

1 teaspoon salt

1 tablespoon freshly chopped rosemary

120 ml/scant ½ cup hot water

2 tablespoons extra virgin olive oil, plus extra for brushing

serves 4

PLANTAIN with lime & chilli/chile

PLANTAIN LENDS ITSELF VERY WELL TO BARBECUES AND GRILL PANS. THE COOKING PROCESS BRINGS OUT ITS SWEETNESS, SO IT'S GOOD TO OFFSET THAT WITH A BIT OF CITRUS AND CHILLI/CHILE. PLANTAIN IS READILY AVAILABLE FROM SOME SUPERMARKETS/STORES OR SPECIALITY CARIBBEAN SHOPS.

★ Put the slices of plantain in a large bowl with the lime juice and chilli/chile oil. Turn them over to coat evenly (this will stop them discolouring).

★ Preheat the barbecue/grill. Arrange the slices on the grill and cook for 2–3 minutes or until slightly charred. Gently turn them over, using a spatula, then cook the other side for 2 minutes.

★ When cooked, lift onto a plate, sprinkle with salt and fresh coriander/cilantro, then serve.

Note: When plantains are at their best for cooking, they have blackened skins and look like ordinary bananas that have gone past their best.

2 plantains, thinly sliced diagonally

freshly squeezed juice of 1 lime

1 tablespoon chilli/chile oil

sea salt

fresh coriander/cilantro, coarsely chopped, to serve

serves 4

CHAPTER 2

SKEWERS & KEBABS

tofu skewers

6 large fresh red chillies/chiles, deseeded and finely chopped

6 garlic cloves, finely chopped

2.5-cm/1-inch piece of root ginger, peeled and finely chopped

½ teaspoon ground white pepper

2 tablespoons cooking sherry or Shaoxing rice wine

2 tablespoons vegan fish sauce (optional)

2 tablespoons dark soy sauce

4 tablespoons agave syrup

1 tablespoon soft brown sugar

½ bunch of fresh coriander/cilantro, leaves and stems chopped

36 tofu puffs

sea salt

sticky rice, to serve (optional)

dipping sauce

¼ cucumber, peeled and halved lengthways

1 teaspoon light soy sauce

3 tablespoons freshly squeezed lime juice

2–3 teaspoons soft brown sugar, to taste

1 tablespoon peanuts, lightly toasted in a dry frying pan/skillet

2 tablespoons rice vinegar

1 red shallot, finely chopped

1 green and 1 red chilli/chile, deseeded and finely chopped

a pinch of salt

12 bamboo skewers, soaked in water for 30 minutes

serves 4–6

STICKY BBQ TOFU SKEWERS

THESE ASIAN-INSPIRED STICKY TOFU SKEWERS ARE TYPICAL OF STREET FOOD YOU MIGHT FIND IN BANGKOK. TRY SERVING WITH STICKY RICE FOR MOPPING UP THE PEANUT AND CUCUMBER DIPPING SAUCE. TOFU PUFFS ARE DEEP-FRIED CUBES OF FIRM TOFU, YOU CAN EITHER MAKE THESE OR BUY THEM PRE-PREPARED FROM CHINESE SUPERMARKETS/STORES.

★ To make the marinade for the tofu, in a large bowl, combine all the ingredients except the tofu puffs. Mix well until all the sugar has dissolved. Season to taste.

★ Put the tofu puffs in the bowl and stir to coat in the marinade. Set aside for at least 1 hour or preferably overnight.

★ For the dipping sauce, use a teaspoon to scrape out the seeds from the centre of the cucumber, then slice the flesh thinly into crescents. Put the soy sauce in a bowl and add the lime juice and sugar. Stir until dissolved. Using a pestle and mortar, grind or crush the peanuts to a rough powder. Add this peanut powder and all the remaining ingredients to the soy sauce mixture and stir well before pouring over the prepared cucumber and tossing to coat in the dressing.

★ Preheat the barbecue/grill. Skewer 3 pieces of puff onto each soaked bamboo skewer. Grill the skewers, turning occasionally, for 10–12 minutes or until golden brown and crispy on the outside. Serve two or three skewers per person with a little pot of the peanut and cucumber dipping sauce. You can also serve them with sticky rice.

GARLIC BREAD SKEWERS

1 baguette

100 ml/⅔ cup extra virgin olive oil

2 garlic cloves, crushed

2 tablespoons freshly chopped flat-leaf parsley

sea salt and freshly ground black pepper

6–8 wooden skewers, soaked in water for 30 minutes

serves 6–8

THIS IS A FUN VERSION OF GARLIC BREAD, AND THE SMOKY FLAVOUR YOU GET FROM THE BARBECUE/GRILL IS DELICIOUS. TRY DUNKING THESE IN ANY OF THE DIPS ON PAGE 11. YOU CAN ALSO ADD CUBES OF CHEESE SUCH AS MOZZARELLA FOR A SERIOUSLY GOOD TREAT.

★ Cut the bread into 2.5-cm/1-inch slices, then cut the slices crossways to make half moons.

★ Put the olive oil, garlic, parsley, salt and pepper in a large bowl, add the bread, and toss until well coated with the parsley and oil.

★ Preheat the barbecue/grill. Thread the garlic bread onto the soaked skewers and cook for 2 to 3 minutes on each side until golden and toasted to your liking.

Variation: Cut 220 g/8 oz. mozzarella into about 24 small pieces. Thread a piece of bread onto the skewer and continue to alternate the cheese and bread. Cook as in the main recipe.

1 large, firm, ripe mango

1 yellow (bell) pepper, deseeded and cut into 10 pieces

2 small red onions, cut into 10 wedges

2 small courgettes/zucchini, cut into 10 pieces

1–2 limes, cut into 10 slices

10 button mushrooms

1 red (bell) pepper, deseeded and cut into 10 pieces

5 chillies/chiles, halved and deseeded (optional)

20 kaffir lime leaves (optional)

Thai barbecue sauce

50 g/1¾ oz. block creamed coconut, chopped

75 ml/scant ⅓ cup dark soy sauce

2 tablespoons soft brown sugar

2 tablespoons rice wine vinegar or freshly squeezed lime juice

3 tablespoons tomato purée/paste

3 kaffir lime leaves, chopped

1 lemongrass stalk, thinly sliced

1–2 red chillies/chiles, sliced

1 garlic clove, sliced

2 tablespoons sunflower oil

10 metal or long bamboo skewers (if bamboo, soak in water for 30 minutes)

makes 10

THAI-GLAZED VEGETABLE SKEWERS

TURN ORDINARY VEGETABLES INTO SOMETHING FABULOUS WITH THIS GORGEOUS THAI-FLAVOURED SAUCE. USE IT AS A MARINADE HERE, BUT ALSO TRY IT AS A KETCHUP FOR BURGERS. THE SAUCE WILL KEEP FOR UP TO A WEEK IN AN AIRTIGHT CONTAINER IN THE REFRIGERATOR.

★ To make the sauce, put the creamed coconut in a bowl, add 3 tablespoons boiling water and dissolve to make a thick paste. Transfer to a blender or food processor, add the remaining sauce ingredients and blend until smooth.

★ Peel the mango with a sharp knife and stand it upright on a board, narrow end pointing up. Slice off thick cheeks parallel to the pit and cut off strips around the pit. Cut the flesh into equal chunks.

★ Thread the skewers with the fruit and vegetable chunks, each starting and ending with a lime leaf, if using. Brush the sauce generously over the loaded skewers, then cover and let marinate in the refrigerator for at least 30 minutes. Reserve the remaining sauce for the next step.

★ Preheat the barbecue/grill. Cook the skewers, turning occasionally and basting with the remaining Thai barbecue sauce, until the vegetables are charred and tender.

CHARGRILLED HALLOUMI
with mixed olive tapenade

- -

250 g/8 oz. halloumi

1 red (bell) pepper, deseeded

1 courgette/zucchini

1 teaspoon coriander seeds

1 teaspoon cumin seeds

1 garlic clove, crushed

½ teaspoon dried oregano

2–3 tablespoons olive oil

sea salt and freshly ground black pepper

toasted flatbreads or pitta breads, to serve

tapenade

4 tablespoons mixed pitted olives

½ small preserved lemon, rind only

2 tablespoons freshly chopped flat-leaf parsley

1 tablespoon freshly chopped mint leaves

1 garlic clove

4 tablespoons fruity extra virgin olive oil

8 wooden skewers, soaked in water for 30 minutes

serves 4

THE SQUEAKY TEXTURE OF HOT, SALTY HALLOUMI CHEESE IS UNIQUELY DELICIOUS. SERVE THESE VIBRANT SKEWERS WITH WARM FLATBREAD OR PITTA BREADS AND A GOOD SPOONFUL OF THE HERBY TAPENADE. THE SKEWERS CAN BE PREPARED IN ADVANCE BUT SHOULD BE EATEN IMMEDIATELY AFTER COOKING.

★ Cut the halloumi into chunks and place in a shallow dish. Cut the red (bell) pepper and courgette/zucchini into chunks the same size as the halloumi and add to the shallow dish.

★ Toast the coriander seeds and cumin seeds in a dry frying pan/skillet over medium heat for about 1 minute, or until aromatic. Crush lightly using a pestle and mortar and add to the halloumi and vegetables. Add the garlic, oregano and olive oil. Season with black pepper, mix well to combine and set aside to marinate for an hour or so.

★ To make the tapenade, tip all the ingredients into a food processor and whiz until combined and roughly chopped. Taste and add black pepper and salt if necessary, but remember that the halloumi is quite salty already.

★ Preheat the barbecue/grill. Thread the marinated halloumi, courgettes/zucchini and (bell) peppers onto the soaked wooden skewers, making sure that each one has an even amount of vegetables and cheese. Cook the skewers on the preheated barbecue/grill in batches until golden and the cheese has softened. Serve with the tapenade and warmed flatbread or pitta breads.

BEET & BABY ONION BROCHETTES

FOR THIS DISH YOU NEED BEET(ROOT) AND BABY ONIONS OF ROUGHLY THE SAME SIZE, SO THEY WILL COOK EVENLY ON THE BARBECUE OR GRILL. THEY ARE FILLING ENOUGH TO BE A MAIN DISH WHEN SERVED ALONGSIDE A POTATO DISH OR THE GRILLED ROSEMARY FLATBREAD (SEE PAGE 27) AND A GORGEOUS SALAD.

32 large fresh bay leaves

20 small beet(root)

20 baby onions, unpeeled

3 tablespoons extra virgin olive oil

1 tablespoon balsamic vinegar

sea salt and freshly ground black pepper

8 metal skewers

serves 4

★ Put the bay leaves in a bowl, cover with cold water and let soak for 1 hour before cooking.

★ Cut the stalks off the beet(root) and wash well under cold running water. Bring a large saucepan of lightly salted water to the boil, add the beet(root) and baby onions and blanch for 5 minutes. Drain and refresh under cold running water. Pat dry with paper towels, then peel the onions.

★ Preheat the barbecue/grill.

★ Thread the beet(root), onions and damp bay leaves onto the metal skewers, sprinkle with the olive oil and vinegar and season well with salt and pepper. Cook on the preheated barbecue/grill for 20–25 minutes, turning occasionally, until charred and tender, then serve immediately. Remember, the metal skewers will be hot so use a kitchen cloth or heat-proof glove when removing from the heat.

SUMMER VEGETABLE KEBABS with pesto

2 aubergines/eggplants, cut into chunks

2 courgettes/zucchini, cut into chunks

2–3 (bell) peppers, stalks removed, deseeded and cut into chunks

12–16 cherry tomatoes

4 red onions, cut into quarters

marinade

4 tablespoons olive oil

freshly squeezed juice of ½ lemon

2 garlic cloves, crushed

1 teaspoon sea salt

pesto

3–4 garlic cloves, roughly chopped

leaves from a large bunch of fresh basil (at least 30–40 leaves)

½ teaspoon sea salt

2–3 tablespoons pine nuts/kernels

extra virgin olive oil, as required

about 60 g/¾ cup freshly grated Italian-style hard cheese

4–6 wooden skewers, soaked in water for 30 minutes

serves 4–6

FULL OF SUNSHINE FLAVOURS, THESE KEBABS CAN BE SERVED WITH COUSCOUS AND A SALAD, OR WITH PASTA TOSSED IN SOME OF THE PESTO SAUCE. HOME-MADE PESTO IS VERY PERSONAL – SOME PEOPLE LIKE IT VERY GARLICKY, OTHERS PREFER LOTS OF BASIL OR CHEESE – SO SIMPLY ADJUST THE QUANTITIES TO SUIT YOUR TASTE.

★ To make the pesto, use a mortar and pestle to pound the garlic with the basil leaves and salt – the salt will act as an abrasive and help to grind. (If you only have a small mortar and pestle, you may have to do this in batches.) Add the pine nuts/kernels and pound them to a paste. Slowly drizzle in some olive oil and bind with the grated Italian-style hard cheese. Continue to pound and grind with the pestle, adding in enough oil to make a smooth sauce. Set aside.

★ Put all the prepared vegetables in a bowl. Mix together the olive oil, lemon juice, garlic and salt and pour it over the vegetables. Using your hands, toss the vegetables gently in the marinade, then thread them onto the soaked skewers.

★ Preheat the barbecue/grill. Cook the kebabs for 2–3 minutes on each side, until the vegetables are charred and tender. Serve the kebabs with the pesto on the side for drizzling.

280 g/10 oz. tofu, rinsed, drained, patted dry and cut into bite-size cubes

leaves from a small bunch of fresh basil, shredded, to serve

sesame oil, for frying

marinade

3 lemongrass stalks, trimmed and finely chopped

1 tablespoon groundnut/peanut oil

3 tablespoons soy sauce

1–2 fresh red chillies/chiles, deseeded and finely chopped

2 garlic cloves, crushed

1 teaspoon ground turmeric

2 teaspoons sugar

sea salt

soy dipping sauce

4–5 tablespoons soy sauce

freshly squeezed juice of 1 lime

1–2 teaspoons sugar

1 fresh red chilli/chile, deseeded and finely chopped

a packet of wooden skewers, soaked in water for 30 minutes

serves 3–4

SPICY TOFU SATAY
with soy dipping sauce

HERE IS A VERY TASTY DISH THAT DOES WONDERFUL THINGS TO TOFU, WHICH CAN BE RATHER BLAND. FULL OF THE FLAVOURS OF SOUTHEAST ASIA, THIS VIETNAMESE DISH IS SOLD AT STREET STALLS AS A SNACK BUT SERVE IT WITH NOODLE SALAD AND ASIAN SLAW AS A MAIN DISH.

★ To make the marinade, mix the lemongrass, groundnut/peanut oil, soy sauce, chilli/chile, garlic and turmeric with the sugar until it has dissolved. Add a little salt to taste and toss in the tofu, making sure it is well coated. Leave to marinate for 1 hour.

★ Prepare the soy dipping sauce by whisking all the ingredients together. Set aside until ready to serve.

★ Preheat the barbecue/grill. Thread the tofu cubes onto the soaked wooden skewers and grill for 2–3 minutes on each side. Serve the tofu hot, garnished with the shredded basil and with the soy dipping sauce on the side.

AUBERGINE/EGGPLANT
with honey & spices

- -

8 aubergines/eggplants, thickly sliced lengthways

olive oil, for brushing

2–3 garlic cloves, crushed

2.5-cm/1-inch piece of root ginger, peeled and finely chopped

1 teaspoon ground cumin

1 teaspoon harissa paste

5 tablespoons runny honey

freshly squeezed juice of 1 lemon

sea salt

a small bunch of fresh flat leaf parsley, finely chopped

couscous (see page 74), to serve

4 wooden skewers, soaked in water for 30 minutes (optional)

serves 4

THIS DELICIOUS DISH WILL SEND YOU ON A MOROCCAN JOURNEY. HOT, SPICY, SWEET AND FRUITY ARE CLASSIC COMBINATIONS OF MIDDLE EASTERN COOKING THAT WORK SO WELL WITH SMOKY GRILLED VEGETABLES. SERVE WITH COUSCOUS (SEE PAGE 74).

★ Preheat the barbecue/grill. Brush each aubergine/eggplant slice with olive oil and cook, turning over so that they are lightly browned.

★ In a wok or large heavy frying pan/skillet, fry the garlic in a little olive oil, then stir in the ginger, cumin, harissa, honey and lemon juice. Add a little water to thin it, then place the aubergine/eggplant slices in the liquid and cook gently for about 10 minutes, until they have absorbed the sauce. Add more water if necessary and season to taste with salt.

★ Thread the aubergines/eggplants onto the soaked skewers, if using, and garnish with the parsley. Serve hot or at room temperature as a meal on their own with couscous, or as an accompaniment to a veggie burger.

1 green (bell) pepper, deseeded and cut into 2.5-cm/1-inch pieces

1 red (bell) pepper, deseeded and cut into 2.5-cm/1-inch pieces

1 onion, cut into 2.5-cm/1-inch pieces

8–10 chestnut mushrooms

1 courgette/zucchini, cut into thick slices

shashlik marinade

2 large red chillies/chiles, trimmed

4 green bird's-eye chillies/chiles, trimmed

6 garlic cloves, peeled and left whole

5-cm/2-inch piece of root ginger, peeled

2 tablespoons vegetable oil

2 teaspoons ground cumin

1 teaspoon ground coriander

1 teaspoon garam masala

½ teaspoon ground turmeric

2 teaspoons ground paprika

½ teaspoon chilli/chili powder

2 tablespoons freshly chopped coriander/cilantro leaves

2 tablespoons tamarind paste

1 tablespoon soft brown sugar

2 tablespoons cornflour/cornstarch

4 tablespoons white wine vinegar

2–3 tablespoons plain yogurt, to taste

salt and freshly ground black pepper

8 bamboo skewers, soaked in water for 30 minutes

serves 4

SHASHLIK SKEWERS

THE SHASHLIK CURRY PASTE ON THESE SKEWERS IS PACKED WITH FLAVOUR, AND IS EXTREMELY VERSATILE. IT CAN EVEN BE USED AS A BASE FOR A CURRY AND WILL KEEP IN THE FRIDGE FOR UP TO A MONTH. SERVE ALONGSIDE RICE PILAF (SEE PAGE 77).

★ Preheat the oven to 220°C (425°F) Gas 7.

★ To make the shashlik marinade, put the chillies/chiles, garlic and ginger in a roasting pan and drizzle with the vegetable oil. Toss to combine. Roast for 8–10 minutes or until well browned. Remove from the oven and cool slightly.

★ Toast the ground spices in a dry frying pan/skillet over high heat for 2 minutes, stirring occasionally, to release the aroma. Put in a small food processor with the roasted chillies/chiles, garlic and ginger, add the fresh coriander/cilantro, tamarind paste, sugar, cornflour/cornstarch and vinegar, and blend until smooth. Season with salt and pepper.

★ Put 4 tablespoons of the marinade in a bowl and stir in the yogurt (you can make it less spicy by adding more yogurt). Add the vegetables, tossing to make sure all the pieces are well coated. Cover the bowl with clingfilm/plastic wrap and chill in the refrigerator for at least 20 minutes.

★ Preheat the barbecue/grill. Cook the vegetable skewers for 5–6 minutes on each side until charred and tender.

CHAPTER 3

POCKETS & BURGERS

HALLOUMI PITTA POCKETS

WHO DOESN'T LOVE HALLOUMI? IT'S THE SALTINESS AND THAT SQUEAK. IF YOU'VE GOT HALLOUMI IN THE FRIDGE IT WILL LAST FOR MONTHS IN THERE, READY TO SIMPLY SLICE AND THROW ON THE BARBECUE OR GRILL AT A MOMENT'S NOTICE. THE SALTINESS GOES SO WELL WITH SOME DELICIOUSLY CHARRED AND WELL-SEASONED VEGETABLES; MAKING A SIMPLE, NOURISHING MEAL THAT EVERYONE WILL ENJOY.

1 courgette/zucchini

2 roasted red (bell) peppers from a jar

125 g/4 oz. halloumi

a handful of pitted black olives

a small handful of fresh flat-leaf parsley, chopped

4 mini pitta breads

salt and freshly ground black pepper

hummus, to serve

freshly squeezed lemon juice, to serve

serves 2

★ Top and tail the courgette/zucchini, slice into thirds, and slice each third lengthways, each strip as thick as a pound coin (⅛ inch). Put in a shallow bowl with some olive oil.

★ Drain the (bell) peppers from the jar. Remove any seeds and slice slightly smaller than the courgette/zucchini. Put in the same shallow bowl and make sure everything is thoroughly covered in oil.

★ Preheat the barbecue/grill. Once it's hot, place the courgette/zucchini and (bell) peppers on the grill. Season with salt and pepper.

★ After a minute or so, check one of the courgettes/zucchini or (bell) peppers and if they are done, turn over and cook on the other side for a minute or so. Season. Remove from the heat.

★ Cut the halloumi into four slices 1.5 cm (¾ inch) thick; at this thickness, they are less likely to fall apart. One slice will go into each pitta pocket.

★ Grill the pittas lightly on each side for a minute either under a grill/broiler or on the barbecue/grill. Put the halloumi in the shallow bowl and make sure the surfaces get covered in oil. Place on the hot barbecue/grill. Leave for about 30 seconds, until charred lines appear, and then turn.

★ Cut open the pittas and stuff with the courgette/zucchini, (bell) peppers, olives, chopped parsley and hot halloumi. Serve with hummus and a squeeze of lemon juice.

a handful of fresh dill, finely chopped

a handful of fresh flat-leaf parsley leaves, finely chopped

leaves from 2 sprigs of fresh thyme

225 g/1¾ cups beet(root), grated

150 g/1¼ cups carrot, finely grated

120 g/¾ cup oatmeal

3 eggs

1 small red onion, finely chopped

2 garlic cloves, crushed

sea salt and freshly ground black pepper

1 tablespoon vegetable oil

bread rolls, split in half

to serve

rocket/arugula leaves

cherry tomatoes, halved

slaw

wholegrain mustard mayonnaise

300 ml/2 cups extra virgin olive oil

300 ml/2 cups sunflower oil

2 egg yolks

1 teaspoon Dijon mustard

freshly squeezed lemon juice, to taste

3 teaspoons wholegrain mustard

makes about 10

BEET BURGERS
with wholegrain mustard mayonnaise

THERE IS NO QUESTION THAT REDUCING THE AMOUNT OF MEAT IN YOUR DIET IS NOT ONLY A HEALTHY CHOICE BUT ALSO GOOD FOR THE PLANET. THIS IS NOT AN ATTEMPT TO REPLICATE A BEEF BURGER BUT IT HAS A SATISFYING TEXTURE THAT GOES DOWN WELL WITH CARNIVORES.

★ Thoroughly combine the herbs, beet(root), carrot, oatmeal, eggs, onion and garlic in a bowl, making sure the eggs and herbs are evenly distributed. Season with 1 teaspoon salt and a few grindings of pepper. Set aside for 15 minutes.

★ To make the wholegrain mustard mayonnaise, you can use a food processor or an electric whisk. Either way, combine the oils in a jug/pitcher. Put the egg yolks, Dijon mustard, lemon juice and a pinch of salt in the food processor bowl or a mixing bowl. As you start to process/whisk, very slowly feed in the oils a little at a time until the mixture begins to emulsify and come together. Once this happens you can add the oil a bit faster, but never be tempted to pour it all in otherwise the mayonnaise will split. Once you have added all the oil, stir in the wholegrain mustard and refrigerate until needed.

★ Preheat the barbecue/grill and preheat the oven to 180°C (350°F) Gas 4.

★ To make the burgers, form about 10 patties with your hands. Cook on the preheated barbecue/grill until browned – 2–3 minutes on each side. Transfer to an ovenproof dish and bake in the preheated oven for 20 minutes.

★ Quickly toast the split bread rolls on the barbecue/grill. Spread the wholegrain mustard mayonnaise on the inside. Add the rocket/arugula, some halved tomatoes, some slaw and a burger.

SPICED FALAFEL BURGERS

225 g/1¼ cups dried chickpeas

1 small onion, finely chopped

2 garlic cloves, crushed

½ bunch of fresh flat leaf parsley

½ bunch of fresh coriander/cilantro

2 teaspoons ground coriander

½ teaspoon baking powder

4 soft oval rolls, split in half

sea salt and freshly ground black pepper

sunflower oil, for shallow frying

salad leaves, to serve

diced tomatoes, to serve

tahini yogurt sauce

100 ml/½ cup thick Greek or plain yogurt

1 tablespoon tahini paste

1 garlic clove, crushed

½ tablespoon freshly squeezed lemon juice

1 tablespoon extra virgin olive oil

serves 4

SO MANY HERBS AND SPICES CAN BE STUFFED INTO CHICKPEA FALAFEL PATTIES. THEY ARE TRADITIONALLY SERVED IN A PITTA WITH HUMMUS. HERE, A TANGY AND SMOOTH TAHINI YOGURT DRESSING IS USED INSTEAD ALONG WITH A SOFT ROLL. FRY THESE BURGERS FIRST TO PREVENT THEM FROM BECOMING DRY, AND FINISH OFF COOKING ON THE BARBECUE OR GRILL TO GIVE A WONDERFUL CHARGRILLED FLAVOUR.

★ Put the dried chickpeas in a bowl and add cold water to cover by a good 12 cm/5 inches. Let soak overnight. Drain the chickpeas well, transfer to a food processor and blend until coarsely ground. Add the onion, garlic, parsley, fresh coriander/cilantro and ground coriander, baking powder and some salt and pepper and blend until very smooth. Transfer to a bowl, cover and chill for 30 minutes.

★ To make the tahini sauce, put the yogurt, tahini, garlic, lemon juice and olive oil in a bowl and whisk until smooth. Season to taste with salt and pepper and set aside until required.

★ Preheat the barbecue/grill. Using wet hands, shape the chickpea mixture into 12 small or 8 medium patties. Heat a shallow layer of sunflower oil in a frying pan/skillet, add the patties and fry for 3 minutes on each side. Drain on paper towels. Place the patties on the barbecue/grill for a few minutes to impart a smoky flavour.

★ Fill the rolls with 2–3 patties, tahini yogurt sauce, salad leaves and diced tomato. Serve hot.

MUSHROOM BURGERS
with chilli/chile mayonnaise & red onion jam

A JUICY PORTOBELLO MUSHROOM IS JUST THE TICKET FOR PEOPLE WHO DON'T EAT MEAT BUT LOVE A GOOD BURGER. THE RED ONION JAM CAN BE MADE AHEAD AND KEPT IN THE REFRIGERATOR FOR SEVERAL DAYS.

1 large red chilli/chile

about 115 g/½ cup mayonnaise

2 tablespoons extra virgin olive oil

4 large portobello mushrooms, stems trimmed

4 burger buns, split in half

sea salt and freshly ground black pepper

salad leaves, to serve

red onion jam

2 tablespoons olive oil

2 red onions, thinly sliced

80 g/¼ cup redcurrant jelly

1 tablespoon red wine vinegar

serves 4

★ To make the red onion jam, heat the olive oil in a saucepan, add the onions and sauté gently for 15 minutes or until very soft. Add a pinch of salt, the redcurrant jelly, vinegar and 2 tablespoons water and cook for another 15 minutes or until the mixture is glossy with a jam-like consistency. Remove from the heat and let cool.

★ Preheat the barbecue/grill. Cook the chilli/chile whole over high heat for 1–2 minutes or until the skin is charred and blackened. Transfer to a plastic bag, seal and let cool slightly. Peel the chilli/chile, then remove and discard the seeds. Chop the flesh and transfer to a food processor. Add the mayonnaise and process until the sauce is speckled red. Taste and adjust the seasoning with salt and pepper, if necessary.

★ Brush the olive oil over the mushrooms, season well with salt and pepper, and cook on the hot barbecue/grill, stem side down, for 5 minutes. Using a spatula, flip the mushrooms and cook them on the other side for about 5 minutes until they are tender.

★ Toast the split buns for a few minutes on the barbecue/grill, then fill them with the mushrooms, salad leaves, onion jam and a spoonful of the chilli/chile mayonnaise.

QUINOA BURGERS
with portobello mushroom 'buns'

3 tablespoons olive oil

1 onion, finely chopped

2 garlic cloves, crushed

75 g/½ cup black beans

120 g/1 cup cooked quinoa

100 g/½ cup cooked sweet potato flesh

1 carrot, shredded

½ teaspoon ground cumin

½ teaspoon ground coriander

2 tablespoons freshly chopped flat-leaf parsley

15 g/⅛ cup breadcrumbs

5 portobello mushrooms

a pinch each of sea salt and freshly ground black pepper

to serve

avocado, sliced

tomato, sliced

gherkins/pickles, chopped

red onion, sliced

fresh coriander/cilantro

freshly squeezed lime juice

a baking sheet, lined with baking parchment

serves 5

THIS VEGGIE BURGER IS A MUST-HAVE RECIPE! MOIST QUINOA MIXES WITH SWEET POTATO AND BLACK BEANS FOR A FILLING CONSISTENCY. GRILLED MUSHROOM 'BUNS' ARE THE PERFECT ACCOMPANIMENT.

★ Preheat the oven to 180°C (350°F) Gas 4.

★ Heat 1 tablespoon of the olive oil in a saucepan over medium heat. Fry the onions for about 3 minutes, until softened. Add the garlic and cook for another minute. Then add the black beans, stir and cook for a few minutes longer. Remove from the heat and transfer the mixture to a large bowl.

★ Lightly mash the beans with a fork until they're semi-crushed. Add the rest of the ingredients (except the mushrooms and remaining olive oil) to the bowl and mix well. If the mixture is too moist, add extra breadcrumbs. If too dry, add some more smashed beans. Form patties with your hands and place on the lined baking sheet. Bake in the preheated oven for 20–25 minutes, checking after about 15 minutes and turning once to ensure even browning.

★ Preheat the barbecue/grill.

★ Remove the burgers from the main oven and place on the barbecue/grill for a few minutes to impart a smoky flavour.

★ For the mushroom 'bun', clean the mushrooms with a damp cloth. Remove the stems and drizzle with the remaining 2 tablespoons olive oil. Season with salt and pepper and grill the mushrooms for 5 minutes on either side.

★ When ready to serve, place each burger on top of a roasted mushroom and garnish with avocado, tomato, gherkins/pickles, red onion, coriander/cilantro and lime juice to taste.

CHUNKY AUBERGINE/EGGPLANT BURGERS

1 large aubergine/eggplant

4 tablespoons extra virgin olive oil

1 tablespoon balsamic vinegar

1 garlic clove, crushed

sea salt and freshly ground black pepper

4 soft bread rolls, split in half

1 quantity pesto (see page 38)

to serve

2 beefsteak tomatoes, thickly sliced

200 g/7 oz. mozzarella cheese, sliced

rocket/arugula leaves

serves 4

THE SMOKY TASTE OF CHARGRILLED AUBERGINE/EGGPLANT AND THE BASIL PESTO GIVE THESE BURGERS A DISTINCTIVE MEDITERRANEAN FLAVOUR. YOU COULD REPLACE THE FRESH BEEFSTEAK TOMATOES WITH SUNDRIED TOMATOES TO TAKE THE THEME EVEN FURTHER, IF YOU LIKE.

★ Preheat the barbecue/grill.

★ Cut the aubergine/eggplant into roughly 1 cm/½ inch slices. Put the oil, vinegar, garlic, salt and pepper in a bowl, whisk to mix, then brush over the aubergine/eggplant slices. Cook them on the preheated barbecue/grill for 3–4 minutes on each side until charred and tender.

★ Lightly toast the split rolls on the barbecue/grill and top with a slice of the charred aubergine/eggplant. Spread with pesto, add another slice of aubergine/eggplant, then add a slice each of tomato and mozzarella. Drizzle with more pesto, then top with rocket/arugula leaves. Put the tops on the rolls and serve hot.

CURRIED SWEET POTATO BURGERS

75 g/½ cup bulgur wheat

400 g/14 oz. sweet potatoes, cubed

1½ tablespoons olive oil, plus extra for shallow frying

1 small onion, finely chopped

1 garlic clove, crushed

1 tablespoon curry powder

75 g/½ cup blanched almonds, finely chopped

2 tablespoons freshly chopped coriander/cilantro

1 egg, lightly beaten

4 tablespoons plain/all purpose flour

4 burger buns, split in half

sea salt and freshly ground black pepper

to serve

salad leaves

cucumber, sliced

mango chutney

lime pickle

plain yogurt

serves 4

ADDING SOME LIME PICKLE AND MANGO CHUTNEY TO THESE NUTTY BURGERS GOES SO WELL WITH THE CURRIED SWEET POTATO. USE PLAIN BUNS OR EVEN WARM CHAPATTI TO WRAP THEM UP. BULGUR IS A CRACKED WHEAT AVAILABLE FROM SUPERMARKETS AND HEALTH FOOD STORES.

★ Put the bulgur wheat in a heatproof bowl, add boiling water to cover by 3 cm/1¼ inch and set aside to soak for 20 minutes until tender. Drain well.

★ Meanwhile, steam the potatoes for 10–15 minutes until cooked. Drain well and mash with a potato masher. Heat the olive oil in a frying pan/skillet and fry the onion, garlic and curry powder for 10 minutes until the onion is soft.

★ Put the bulgur wheat, mashed potato, onion mixture, almonds, coriander/cilantro, egg, flour and some salt and pepper in a bowl. Work together with your hands until evenly mixed. Cover and chill for 30 minutes. Using wet hands, divide the mixture into 8 portions and shape into patties.

★ Preheat the barbecue/grill.

★ Heat a shallow layer of olive oil in a frying pan/skillet, add the patties and fry gently for 3–4 minutes on each side until golden. Transfer the patties to the hot barbecue/grill and cook for a minute on each side to impart smoky flavour. Toast the split buns on the barbecue/grill and fill with the patties, salad leaves, cucumber slices and mango chutney. Top with some lime pickle and yogurt, if using, and serve hot.

SPICY VEGAN BURGERS

- -

MAKING A GOOD VEGAN BURGER IS A TRICKY BUSINESS, BUT THESE ARE THE ANSWER! DEEP-FRIED TO GET A NICE CRISP CRUST AND A JUICY INSIDE, THEY HAVE A BARBECUE FLAVOUR TO THEM WHICH COMES FROM THE SPICE MIX AND FLAVOURINGS INSIDE.

80 g/¾ cup vegetable pulp or grated root vegetables such as carrot or swede

50 g/⅓ cup finely diced onion

3 garlic cloves, crushed

1 teaspoon barbecue spice mix

¼ teaspoon sweet paprika

¼ teaspoon ground turmeric

⅛ teaspoon chilli/chili powder

4 tablespoons freshly chopped herbs (parsley, chives, etc.)

575 g/3⅓ cups cooked brown rice, room temperature

¾ teaspoon sea salt

plain/all-purpose flour, for coating

sunflower oil, for frying

to serve

sweet potato wedges

gherkins/pickles, sliced

red onion, sliced

tofu mayonnaise

serves 4–5

★ For the burgers, put all the ingredients (except the flour and the oil) in a big bowl. Using your hands, knead the rice into the mixture until everything is well combined and the rice starts becoming sticky. This will prevent the burgers from falling apart or absorbing too much oil. Taste and add more salt and spice if needed. Allow the mixture to rest for 30 minutes.

★ With moist hands, shape the mixture into small patties – you should be able to make about 14. Roll each burger in a little flour and set aside.

★ Meanwhile, fill a deep, heavy-bottomed frying pan/skillet with 3 cm/1¼ inches of vegetable oil and heat it until the oil starts moving. To tell if it's the right temperature, throw a small piece of the mixture into the pan: if it immediately starts boiling, it's ready to go. Deep-fry a couple of burgers at a time, depending on the size of your pan – it should not be overcrowded. When they turn golden brown, remove them from the oil with a slotted spoon and place them on paper towels. They should be golden with a thin crust and a juicy inside, and should only grease your fingers lightly.

★ Serve the burgers hot with sweet potato wedges, gherkins/pickles, onion slices and tofu mayonnaise.

GRILLED VEGETABLE BURGERS
with halloumi 'buns'

ROASTED VEGETABLES AND HALLOUMI ARE A WONDERFUL COMBINATION OF TASTES AND TEXTURES. USING HALLOUMI AS AN ALTERNATIVE TO A BREADY 'BUN' MAKES A TOTALLY DELICIOUS BUT CARB-FREE MEAL – GREAT FOR THOSE WHO PREFER OR REQUIRE A GLUTEN-FREE DIET.

1 large aubergine/eggplant

3 small courgettes/zucchini, any colour

1 large red onion

2 red (bell) peppers

3–4 tablespoons olive oil

3 large sprigs of rosemary

freshly squeezed juice of ½ lemon

2 x 250-g/9-oz. blocks of halloumi, sliced

sea salt and freshly ground black pepper

cocktail sticks/toothpicks

serves 6

★ Preheat the oven to 220°C (425°F) Gas 7.

★ Slice the aubergine/eggplant and the courgettes/zucchini widthways into 1-cm/½-inch thick slices. Peel and chop the onion into thick wedges. Lastly, chop the (bell) peppers in half, remove the seeds and cut into 1-cm/½-inch thick strips. Drizzle a little olive oil on a baking sheet and arrange the vegetables with the rosemary sprigs on top. Drizzle over more olive oil, making sure there is plenty on the aubergine/eggplant slices as they tend to dry out in the oven, and season very well with salt and pepper. Roast in the preheated oven for 30–40 minutes, until the vegetables are tender. Leave to cool before squeezing the lemon juice lightly over the vegetables.

★ Preheat the barbecue/grill. Cut the halloumi lengthways into around 6 slices per block and cook for 30 seconds on each side until lightly charred lines appear.

★ To assemble, start with a slice of halloumi on the bottom and layer up your vegetables and 1 further slice of halloumi to top the stack. Secure with cocktail sticks/toothpicks to keep the 'burgers' together, but remember to remove them before serving!

OPEN TOFU BEAN BURGERS

TO ADD EXTRA FLAVOUR TO THESE BURGERS, LOOK OUT FOR VARIETIES OF TOFU THAT COME MARINATED OR SMOKED. BOTH ARE READILY AVAILABLE FROM LARGER SUPERMARKETS AND HEALTH FOOD STORES. THESE PATTIES GO EXTRA CRISP IF YOU FRY THEN GRILL THEM.

2 tablespoons olive oil

1 onion, chopped

1 garlic clove, crushed

2 teaspoons ground coriander

1 teaspoon ground cumin

420-g/15-oz. can red kidney beans, drained

200 g/7 oz. marinated or smoked tofu, rinsed, drained, patted dry and cut into bite-size cubes

75 g/1¼ cups fresh wholemeal/whole-wheat breadcrumbs

50 g/¼ cup crunchy peanut butter

2 tablespoons freshly chopped coriander/cilantro

1 egg, lightly beaten

sea salt and freshly ground black pepper

plain/all-purpose flour, for dusting

2 wholemeal/whole-wheat burger buns, split in half

groundnut/peanut oil, for shallow frying

fresh herbs, to serve

sweet chilli/chile sauce, to serve

serves 4

★ Heat the olive oil in a frying pan/skillet, add the onion, garlic and spices and fry gently for 10 minutes until the onion is softened but not browned. Let cool. Transfer the onion mixture to a food processor, add the beans, tofu, breadcrumbs, peanut butter, coriander/cilantro, egg, salt and pepper and blend until smooth. Transfer the mixture to a bowl, cover and chill for 30 minutes.

★ Using wet hands, divide the mixture into 8 portions and shape into patties. Dust them lightly with flour. Heat a shallow layer of groundnut/peanut oil in a frying pan/skillet, add the patties and fry for 3–4 minutes on each side until crisp and heated through.

★ Preheat the barbecue/grill. Cook the tofu burgers for a few minutes on each side to impart extra smoky flavour.

★ Lightly toast the split buns on the barbecue/grill and top each half with 2 patties, fresh herbs and some sweet chilli/chile sauce. Serve hot.

MUSHROOM BARLEY BURGERS

65 g/⅓ cup barley, rinsed and drained

1 slice wholemeal/whole-wheat bread

1 small onion

2 tablespoons extra virgin olive oil

225 g/1¾ cups mushrooms, trimmed and halved

leaves from a few sprigs of fresh flat-leaf parsley

2 eggs

1 tablespoon soy sauce or tamari

50 g/½ cup grated Cheddar

1 tablespoon unsalted butter

sea salt and freshly ground black pepper

9 wholemeal/whole-wheat buns or rolls

to serve

lettuce leaves

tomato, sliced

ketchup

mayonnaise

pickles

makes 9 burgers

THESE TASTY BURGERS ARE GREAT FOR FEEDING A HUNGRY CROWD OF FRIENDS, THE SIMPLE INGREDIENTS GO A LONG WAY AND BARLEY IS A GREAT TEXTURE FOR A BURGER, FIRM AND PLEASANTLY CHEWY. SERVE WITH ALL THE USUAL BURGER TRIMMINGS.

★ Put the barley in a saucepan and add cold water to cover well. Add a pinch of salt and bring to the boil. Reduce the heat and simmer until tender, about 35–45 minutes. Drain and set aside.

★ Put the slice of bread in a food processor and process to obtain crumbs. Transfer to a bowl and set aside until needed.

★ Put the onion in the food processor and process to chop finely. Transfer to a non-stick frying pan/skillet, add 1 tablespoon of the oil and cook over low heat until soft.

★ Put the mushrooms and parsley in the food processor and process until finely chopped. Set aside until needed.

★ Crack the eggs into a mixing bowl, add a good pinch of salt and beat. Add the mushroom mixture, cooked barley, onions, breadcrumbs, soy sauce and cheese and mix well.

★ Preheat the barbecue/grill. Heat the butter and remaining oil in a large non-stick frying pan/skillet. Working in batches, drop clementine-size balls of the mushroom mixture into the pan and squash gently to flatten with the back of a spatula. Cook on one side for 3 minutes, until browned, then turn over and cook on the other side for 3 minutes more. Transfer the burgers to the hot barbecue/grill and finish off the cooking process there for a further minute on each side. Serve hot in a bun with all the trimmings.

CHEESY ROOT VEGETABLE BURGERS

⅓ butternut squash, peeled and chopped

1 sweet potato, peeled and chopped

1 small potato, peeled and chopped

1 carrot, peeled and chopped

½ red onion, chopped

1 garlic clove, chopped

a large pinch of dried thyme

40 g/⅓ cup grated mature/sharp Cheddar cheese

a pinch of sea salt and freshly ground black pepper

Wholegrain Mustard Mayonnaise (see page 46)

mixed leaf salad, to serve

makes 2 burgers

THESE HEARTY VEGETARIAN BURGERS DON'T REQUIRE A BUN BECAUSE THEY ARE PACKED FULL OF YUMMY ROOT VEGETABLES. SERVE WITH WHOLEGRAIN MUSTARD MAYONNAISE (SEE PAGE 46).

★ Bring a large saucepan of water to the boil. Put the squash, sweet potato, potato, carrot, onion and garlic and boil for about 10 minutes until soft. Strain and mash well with a potato masher. Add the thyme and salt and pepper and work together with your hands until evenly mixed.

★ Divide the mixture in half and shape into two burger patties. Press each burger down to make them nice and flat and roll each one in the cheese, so that it sticks all around the outside of the burger.

★ Preheat the barbecue/grill and the grill/broiler to medium–hot.

★ Put the burgers on a greased baking sheet and grill/broil for 2–3 minutes on each side until the cheese is bubbling. Remove from the grill/broiler and place on the hot barbecue/grill for 3–4 minutes until nicely browned.

★ Let cool slightly and serve with the Wholegrain Mustard Mayonnaise and a mixed leaf salad.

CHAPTER 4

HOT SIDES

GRILLED COURGETTES/ ZUCCHINI

SO SIMPLE YET SO GOOD. COURGETTES/ZUCCHINI ARE THE PERFECT VEGETABLES TO PUT ON A HOT BARBECUE/ GRILL. THEY HOLD THEIR SHAPE WELL, YET THE FLESH TENDERIZES AND CHARS BEAUTIFULLY, SOAKING UP ANY SEASONINGS LIKE A SPONGE. A FEW MINUTES AND YOU WILL HAVE A TASTY HOT SIDE READY TO GO!

8 courgettes/zucchini, cut lengthways into 1-cm/¾-inch slices

olive oil

balsamic vinegar

sea salt and freshly ground black pepper

serves 8

★ Preheat the barbecue/grill.

★ Cook the courgette/zucchini slices for 3–4 minutes on each side, until lightly charred and tender. Remove to a plate and sprinkle with oil, vinegar, salt and pepper. Serve hot, warm or cold.

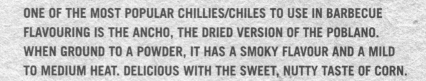

GRILLED CORN with chilli/chile-salt rub

6 cobs/ears of (sweet)corn, husks removed

2 tablespoons extra virgin olive oil, plus extra to serve

3 ancho chillies/chiles

1½ tablespoons sea salt, plus extra for cooking the corn

3 limes, cut into wedges

serves 6

ONE OF THE MOST POPULAR CHILLIES/CHILES TO USE IN BARBECUE FLAVOURING IS THE ANCHO, THE DRIED VERSION OF THE POBLANO. WHEN GROUND TO A POWDER, IT HAS A SMOKY FLAVOUR AND A MILD TO MEDIUM HEAT. DELICIOUS WITH THE SWEET, NUTTY TASTE OF CORN.

★ Trim the ends of the (sweet)corn. Bring a large saucepan of lightly salted water to the boil, add the (sweet)corn, and boil for 1–2 minutes. Drain and refresh under cold water. Pat dry with paper towels.

★ Preheat the barbecue/grill. Brush the (sweet)corn with oil and cook for 5–7 minutes, turning frequently until charred all over.

★ Meanwhile, remove the stalk and seeds from the ancho chillies/chiles. Chop the flesh coarsely and, using a spice grinder or mortar and pestle, grind to a powder. Transfer to a small bowl, then mix in the salt.

★ Rub the lime wedges vigorously over the (sweet)corn, sprinkle with the chilli/chile salt, and serve with extra oil for drizzling.

EMBER-ROASTED POTATOES

A CLASSIC BARBECUE/GRILL SIDE, GREAT FOR FESTIVE FIREWORK PARTIES OR CAMPSITE COOKOUTS. THE SKIN SHOULD BE CRISPY AND THE INTERIOR SOFT AND FLUFFY. ROUGH THE SOFT INSIDE UP FURTHER WITH A FORK AND ADD A HEAP OF GRATED CHEESE OR EAT SIMPLY SLATHERED IN BUTTER AND SALT AND PEPPER.

4 medium roasting potatoes, such as King Edward or Desirée

butter

sea salt and freshly ground black pepper

serves 4

★ Preheat the barbecue/grill.

★ Wrap the potatoes individually in a double layer of kitchen foil and, as soon as the coals glow red, put the potatoes on top. Rake the charcoal up and around them, but without covering them. Let cook for about 25 minutes, then using tongs, turn the potatoes over carefully and cook for a further 25–30 minutes until cooked through.

★ Remove from the heat and carefully remove the ktichen foil, then cut the potatoes in half. Serve, topped with butter, salt and pepper.

SESAME SWEET POTATO PACKETS

SWEET POTATOES ARE PERFECT FOR THE BARBECUE OR GRILL BECAUSE THEY COOK QUICKLY WITHOUT PRE-BOILING. WHEN TOSSED IN DRESSING AND WRAPPED IN KITCHEN FOIL, THE POTATOES STEAM-COOK AND ABSORB THE FLAVOURS OF THE DRESSING. CARE MUST BE TAKEN SO THAT THE POTATOES DO NOT BURN THROUGH THE FOIL WHERE THEY ARE IN DIRECT CONTACT WITH THE HEAT. THIS RECIPE CALLS FOR INDIVIDUAL PACKETS, BUT ONE LARGE PACKET DOES JUST AS WELL. COOK THEM FIRST AND THEN PUT THEM ON ONE SIDE OF THE BARBECUE/GRILL TO KEEP WARM.

4 large sweet potatoes, peeled and cut into 4 or 5 slices

1–2 tablespoons vegetable oil

1–2 tablespoons shoyu or tamari soy sauce

1 tablespoon sesame seeds

1 tablespoon freshly chopped flat-leaf parsley, to serve

serves 4

★ Preheat the barbecue/grill.

★ Put the sweet potato slices in a bowl with the oil, soy sauce and sesame seeds and toss well. Divide between 4 large squares of kitchen foil, then crinkle the foil up around them and close tightly. Put the foil packets on the hot barbecue/grill, close the lid and leave to cook for 20–30 minutes or until tender.

★ When ready to serve, open up the packets and sprinkle a little parsley on the sweet potatoes.

SWEET POTATO WEDGES

---

2 sweet potatoes, unpeeled, sliced into wedges

olive oil, for drizzling

sea salt and freshly ground black pepper

cajun spice rub (optional)

ketchup, for dipping

a baking sheet, greased

serves 2

THE ESSENTIAL MODERN ACCOMPANIMENT TO ANY VEGGIE BURGER IS THE SWEET POTATO WEDGE. YOU CAN KEEP THIS HEALTHY HOT SIDE COOKING IN THE OVEN WHILE THE GRILL OUTSIDE IS CROWDED WITH BURGERS, SKEWERS AND OTHER DELIGHTS.

★ Preheat the oven to 180°C (350°F) Gas 4.

★ Bring a large saucepan of water to the boil. Add the sweet potatoes and boil for about 5 minutes. Remove the potatoes from the pan and lay on the greased baking sheet.

★ Drizzle some olive oil over the top, sprinkle with black pepper and cajun spice rub, if using, and mix to coat.

★ Bake in the preheated oven for 25 minutes until brown and crisp. Shake the baking sheet frequently to make sure the wedges brown evenly without sticking.

★ Remove from the oven, sprinkle with salt and serve immediately with plenty of ketchup for dipping.

CLASSIC HOMECUT FRIES

THERE ARE SOME KIDS THAT WON'T EAT A BURGER WITHOUT CLASSIC HOMECUT FRIES, PROBABLY SOME ADULTS TOO! BAKING RATHER THAN DEEP-FRYING STILL GIVES GREAT FLAVOUR BUT IS SLIGHTLY HEALTHIER. SERVE WITH CLASSIC DIPS OF YOUR CHOOSING.

2 floury potatoes, sliced into fries

olive oil, for drizzling

sea salt and freshly ground black pepper

a baking sheet, greased

serves 2

★ Preheat the oven to 180°C (350°F) Gas 4.

★ Bring a large saucepan of water to the boil. Add the potatoes and boil for about 5 minutes. Remove from the pan and lay on the greased baking sheet.

★ Drizzle some olive oil over the top, sprinkle with salt and pepper, to taste, and mix to coat. Bake in the preheated oven for 25 minutes until golden and crisp.

★ Shake the baking sheet frequently to make sure the fries brown evenly without sticking.

★ Remove from the oven, sprinkle with salt and serve immediately.

CHARRED LEEKS with tarator sauce

TARATOR, THE NUT SAUCE SERVED WITH THESE LEEKS, IS FOUND IN MIDDLE EASTERN COOKING. IT COMPLEMENTS THE SMOKY, CHARGRILLED VEGETABLES PERFECTLY AND COULD ALSO BE USED TO DRIZZLE OVER GRILLED AUBERGINE/EGGPLANT.

750 g/1½ lb. baby leeks, trimmed

2–3 tablespoons extra virgin olive oil

sea salt

a few lemon wedges, to serve

tarator sauce

50 g/2 oz. macadamia nuts, toasted

25 g/scant ½ cup fresh breadcrumbs

2 garlic cloves, crushed

100 ml/⅔ cup extra virgin olive oil

1 tablespoon freshly squeezed lemon juice

2 tablespoons boiling water

sea salt and freshly ground black pepper

serves 4

★ To make the sauce, put the nuts in a food processor and blend coarsely, then add the breadcrumbs, garlic, salt and pepper and process again to form a smooth paste. Transfer to a bowl and very gradually whisk in the olive oil, lemon juice and the 2 tablespoons boiling water to form a sauce. Season to taste with salt and pepper.

★ Preheat the barbecue/grill.

★ Brush the leeks with a little olive oil, season with salt and cook for 6–10 minutes on the hot barbecue/grill, turning occasionally, until charred and tender. Transfer to a serving plate, sprinkle with olive oil, then pour the sauce over the top and serve with the lemon wedges.

RATATOUILLE

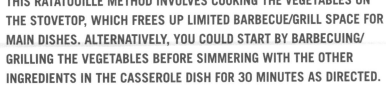

THIS RATATOUILLE METHOD INVOLVES COOKING THE VEGETABLES ON THE STOVETOP, WHICH FREES UP LIMITED BARBECUE/GRILL SPACE FOR MAIN DISHES. ALTERNATIVELY, YOU COULD START BY BARBECUING/ GRILLING THE VEGETABLES BEFORE SIMMERING WITH THE OTHER INGREDIENTS IN THE CASSEROLE DISH FOR 30 MINUTES AS DIRECTED.

1 kg/2¼ lb. aubergines/eggplant, cut into 4-cm/1½-inch pieces

6–7 tablespoons extra virgin olive oil

2 medium onions, roughly chopped

2 red (bell) peppers, halved, deseeded and cut into small chunks

2 yellow (bell) peppers, halved, deseeded and cut into small chunks

1 green (bell) pepper, halved, deseeded and cut into small chunks

6 small courgettes/zucchini, halved lengthways and sliced

4 garlic cloves, crushed

6 medium tomatoes, halved, deseeded and chopped

a small bunch of fresh basil, roughly chopped

sea salt

a few thinly sliced fresh basil leaves, to serve

1 crushed garlic clove, to serve

serves 4–6

★ Put the aubergine/eggplant pieces in a microwave-proof bowl with 3 tablespoons water and microwave on high for 6 minutes. Drain and set aside.

★ Heat 3 tablespoons of the oil in a large casserole dish with a lid. Add the onions and cook until soft, 3–5 minutes. Salt lightly. Add all the (bell) peppers and cook for 5–8 minutes more, stirring often. Turn up the heat to keep the sizzling sound going, but take care not to let it burn. Salt lightly. Add 1 more tablespoon of oil and the courgettes/zucchini. Mix well and cook for about 5 minutes more, stirring occasionally. Salt lightly. Add 2 more tablespoons of oil and the drained aubergines/eggplants. Cook, stirring, for 5 minutes more. Salt lightly. Add the garlic and cook for 1 minute. Add 1 more tablespoon of oil if necessary, and the tomatoes and basil and stir well. Cook for 5 minutes, then cover, lower the heat and simmer gently for 30 minutes, checking occasionally.

★ Remove the casserole from the heat. This is best served at room temperature, but it still tastes good hot. The longer you let it stand, the richer it tastes. Stir in extra basil and garlic just before serving.

ROASTED PUMPKIN WEDGES with lime & spices

THIS IS A GREAT WAY TO ENJOY PUMPKIN. SERVE THESE SPICY WEDGES ON THEIR OWN DRIZZLED WITH COOLING YOGURT, OR WITH ANY OF THE GORGEOUS VEGGIE BURGERS ON PAGES 44–63. SAVE THE PUMPKIN SEEDS AND ROAST THEM LIGHTLY WITH OIL AND SEA SALT AS A NIBBLE.

1 medium-size pumpkin, halved lengthways, deseeded and cut into 6–8 segments

2 teaspoons coriander seeds

1 teaspoon cumin seeds

1 teaspoon fennel seeds

1–2 teaspoons ground cinnamon

2 dried red chillies/chiles, chopped

2 garlic cloves

2 tablespoons olive oil

sea salt

finely grated zest of 1 lime

6 metal skewers, to serve

serves 6

★ Preheat the oven to 200°C (400°F) Gas 6.

★ Using a mortar and pestle, grind all the dried spices with the salt. Add the garlic and a little of the olive oil to form a paste. Rub the mixture over the pumpkin wedges and place them, skin-side down, in a roasting tin. Cook them in the preheated oven for 35–40 minutes, or until tender.

★ Sprinkle over the lime zest and serve hot, threaded onto skewers, if using.

BUTTERY COUSCOUS

THIS IS A BASIC RECIPE TO WHICH YOU CAN ADD
FRESH HERBS, A SPICE PASTE OR PINE NUTS/
KERNELS AND DRIED FRUITS OF YOUR CHOICE.

350 g/2 cups couscous, rinsed and drained
400 ml/1⅔ cups warm water plus ½ teaspoon sea salt
2 tablespoons sunflower or olive oil
25 g/2½ tablespoons butter, cut into small cubes

serves 4–6

★ Preheat the oven to 180°C (350°F) Gas 4.

★ Tip the couscous into an ovenproof dish. Pour the
salted water over the couscous. Leave it to absorb the
water for about 10 minutes. Using your fingers, rub
the oil into the grains to break up the lumps and
aerate them.

★ Scatter the butter over the surface and cover with
a piece of kitchen foil or wet parchment paper. Put in
the preheated oven for 15 minutes to heat through.
Fluff up the grains with a fork before serving.

BULGUR WITH GHEE

BULGUR IS DELICIOUS SERVED WITH KEBABS. YOU
COULD ADD DICED VEGETABLES, SPICES, OR EVEN
POMEGRANATE SEEDS TO THIS BASIC RECIPE.

2 tablespoons ghee or 1 tablespoon olive oil plus a
knob/pat of butter
2 onions, chopped
350 g/1¾ cups bulgur (cracked wheat), thoroughly
rinsed and drained
600 ml/2½ cups vegetable stock or water
sea salt and freshly ground black pepper

serves 4–6

★ Melt the ghee in a heavy-based saucepan. Add the
onions and stir until soft. Add the bulgur, tossing it
thoroughly with the onions.

★ Pour in the stock, season and stir well. Bring to the
boil and cook for 1–2 minutes, then reduce the heat
and simmer, uncovered, until all the liquid has been
absorbed. Turn off the heat, cover the pan with a clean
kitchen cloth, and press a lid on top.

★ Leave to steam for a further 10–15 minutes, then
fluff up with a fork before serving.

SIMPLE NOODLES
with ginger & chilli/chile

THESE SIMPLE NOODLES ARE GOOD SERVED WITH ASIAN FLAVOURS LIKE THE SPICY TOFU SATAY (SEE PAGE 39) AND CAN ALSO FORM THE BASE OF A MORE CREATIVE DISH WITH SHREDDED CABBAGE, CARROT, BEANSPROUTS AND PEANUTS.

225 g/8 oz. dried rice noodles

1–2 tablespoons vegetable oil

2.5-cm/1-inch piece of root ginger, peeled and finely chopped

1–2 red chillies/chiles, deseeded and finely chopped

1–2 garlic cloves, finely chopped

3–4 tablespoons soy sauce

2–3 teaspoons runny honey

1 small bunch of freshly chopped coriander/cilantro leaves

serves 4

★ Soak the noodles in water according to the packet instructions. Heat the oil in a wok or large frying pan/skillet. Add the ginger, chillies/chiles and garlic and stir-fry until fragrant and just beginning to colour.

★ Toss in the reconstituted noodles and add the soy sauce and honey. Stir well. Toss in the chopped coriander/cilantro and serve immediately.

RICE PILAF

THIS RECIPE IS THE BASE TO WHICH OTHER INGREDIENTS, SUCH AS NUTS, GINGER AND COCONUT, CAN BE ADDED. GROUND TURMERIC OR SAFFRON CAN ALSO BE ADDED TO GIVE A LOVELY FRAGRANCE AND VIVID YELLOW COLOUR.

450 g/2½ cups long grain rice, rinsed and soaked in water for 30 minutes

1–2 tablespoons ghee or 1 tablespoon olive oil plus a knob/pat of butter

1 onion, chopped

1 teaspoon sugar

4–6 cardamom pods, bashed to release flavour from the seeds

4 cloves

600 ml/2½ cups water plus 1 teaspoon sea salt

serves 4–6

★ Heat the ghee in a heavy-based saucepan over medium heat. Add the onion and sugar and fry until golden. Add the cardamom pods and cloves and stir in the pre-soaked rice, making sure the grains are coated in the ghee. Pour the salted water over the rice and bring to the boil.

★ Reduce the heat and simmer for 15–20 minutes, uncovered, until the liquid has been absorbed. Turn off the heat, cover the saucepan with a clean kitchen cloth, followed by a lid, and leave the rice to steam for a further 10 minutes before fluffing up and serving.

MIDDLE EASTERN ROASTED VEGETABLES with pomegranate seeds

2 aubergines/eggplants, partially peeled and cut into thin wedges

2 courgettes/zucchini, partially peeled, halved and sliced lengthways or cut into wedges

2 red or yellow (bell) peppers, deseeded and cut into quarters

100–200 ml/⅔–1⅓ cups olive oil

8–10 cherry or baby plum tomatoes

2 firm peaches, peeled, pitted and cut into wedges

1 teaspoon toasted fennel seeds

1 teaspoon toasted coriander seeds

500 g/2 cups thick, creamy yogurt

2–3 garlic cloves, crushed

2 tablespoons pine nuts/kernels

2 tablespoons tahini, well beaten to the consistency of pouring cream

seeds of half a pomegranate

sea salt and freshly ground black pepper

serves 4–6

A MIXED MEZZE FEAST IS THE CLASSIC MIDDLE EASTERN ACCOMPANIMENT TO BARBECUED OR GRILLED FOODS LIKE KEBABS. THIS HOT SIDE DISH (SOMETIMES KNOWN AS 'SHAKSHUKA') HAS AN INTERESTING COMBINATION OF VEGETABLES AND FRUIT. SERVED WITH A GARLICKY YOGURT SAUCE, IT IS A DELICIOUS WAY TO ENJOY VEGETABLES. ADD TO YOUR MIDDLE EASTERN MEZZE THEME WITH THE BABA GHANOUSH AND SWEET POTATO HUMMUS ON PAGE 11.

★ Preheat the oven to 200°C (400°F) Gas 6.

★ Place the aubergines/eggplants, courgettes/zucchini and (bell) peppers in an earthenware or ovenproof dish. Drizzle the oil over them and place them in the preheated oven for 30 minutes, turning them in the oil once or twice. Add the tomatoes, peaches and spices, along with a little extra olive oil if necessary, and return them to the oven for 20 minutes.

★ In a bowl, beat the yogurt with the garlic and season to taste with salt and pepper. In a small heavy-based pan, dry roast the pine nuts/kernels until they give off a nutty aroma and turn golden brown. Tip them into a dish and put aside.

★ When the roasted vegetables are ready, arrange them on a serving dish. Spoon the yogurt over them, drizzle the tahini in swirls and scatter the roasted pine nuts/kernels and pomegranate seeds over the top. Serve while the vegetables are still hot.

FRIED CARROT & FENNEL
with cumin & pomegranate molasses

- -

3 tablespoons olive oil with a knob/pat of butter

2 medium carrots, peeled, halved crossways and cut into long, thin slices

2 small fennel bulbs, trimmed and thinly sliced

2 garlic cloves, crushed

2 teaspoons cumin seeds

1 teaspoon fennel seeds

1–2 teaspoons caster/granulated sugar

the rind of half preserved lemon, finely sliced

2 tablespoons pomegranate molasses

a handful of fresh dill, finely chopped

a handful of fresh flat-leaf parsley, finely chopped

sea salt and freshly ground black pepper

serves 4

FED UP OF PLAIN GRATED CARROTS IN YOUR SALAD? HEARTIER THAN A SALAD BUT LIGHT ENOUGH TO ACCOMPANY HEAVIER GRILLED FOODS, THIS RECIPE IS A PLEASINGLY UNIQUE SIDE DISH TO ADD TO YOUR REPERTOIRE. THE ANISEED FLAVOUR OF FENNEL MARRIES REALLY WELL WITH THE SWEET FRUITY MOLASSES AND SOUR PRESERVED LEMON TO MAKE THE MOST OF THE BEAUTIFUL ROOT VEGETABLES.

★ Heat the olive oil and butter in a wide, heavy-based pan and fry the carrot and fennel for roughly 2 minutes on each side, until they turn nicely golden in colour. Add the garlic, cumin seeds, fennel seeds and sugar and cook for 1–2 minutes, until slightly caramelized.

★ Season well and arrange the carrot and fennel on a serving dish. Scatter the preserved lemon over the top, drizzle with the pomegranate molasses and garnish with the dill and parsley. Serve warm or at room temperature.

TURMERIC POTATOES
with lime & coriander/cilantro

THIS IS ONE POTATO DISH THAT IS PACKED FULL OF FLAVOUR. IT CAN BE SERVED COLD AS PART OF A MEZZE SPREAD OR HOT AS AN ACCOMPANIMENT TO ALMOST ANY BARBECUED OR GRILLED DISH. IT IS EXTREMELY EASY TO PREPARE AND VERY TASTY – THANKS TO THE FLAVOUR OF TURMERIC, A FIERY KICK FROM THE CHILLIES/CHILES AND A REFRESHING BURST OF LIME OR LEMON.

450 g/1 lb. new potatoes

2 tablespoons olive oil with a knob/pat of butter

2–3 garlic cloves, finely chopped

1–2 teaspoons finely chopped dried red chilli/chile or 1 fresh chilli/chile, deseeded and finely chopped

1–2 teaspoons cumin seeds

1–2 teaspoons coriander seeds

2 teaspoons ground turmeric

freshly squeezed juice of 2 limes or lemons

sea salt and freshly ground black pepper

a handful of fresh finely chopped coriander/cilantro, to garnish

serves 4–6

★ Place the potatoes in a steamer with their skins on and steam for about 10-15 minutes, until cooked but still firm. Drain and refresh under cold running water and peel off the skins. Place the potatoes on a wooden board and cut them into bite-size pieces.

★ Heat the olive oil and butter in a heavy-based pan and stir in the garlic, chilli/chile, cumin and coriander seeds for about 2–3 minutes, before adding the turmeric. Toss in the potatoes, coating them in the spices so that they take on the colour of the turmeric. Add the lime juice, making sure it is thoroughly mixed in with the potatoes and spices and, when the pan is almost dry, toss in most of the freshly chopped coriander/cilantro.

★ Season the dish with salt and pepper and garnish with the rest of the coriander/cilantro. Serve hot or at room temperature.

AUBERGINE/EGGPLANT GRATIN

THE VELVETY TEXTURE OF THIS DISH JUST SCREAMS 'BAD FOR YOU', BUT ACTUALLY IT IS PACKED FULL OF VEGETABLES AND USES ONLY A LITTLE CREAM. AUBERGINE/ EGGPLANT IS REALLY SENSATIONAL WHEN SEASONED WELL, SO THIS IS THE PERFECT DISH FOR IT — THE TOMATOES, OIL, AND HERBS REALLY BRING IT TO LIFE. FOR A VEGAN OPTION USE DAIRY-FREE SOYA CREAM INSTEAD OF REGULAR.

2 red onions, sliced

10 ripe cherry tomatoes

extra virgin olive oil

balsamic vinegar

3 aubergines/eggplants, topped, tailed and cut into 1-cm/½-inch slices

a handful of fresh basil leaves

100 ml/6 tablespoons single/ light cream

sea salt and freshly ground black pepper

serves 4–6

★ Preheat the oven to 200°C (400°F) Gas 6.

★ Toss the onions and tomatoes with some oil, salt and a drizzle of balsamic vinegar in an ovenproof dish. Roast in the preheated oven for about 15 minutes or until the skins of the tomatoes crack open and the onions are beginning to caramelize. Leave the oven on.

★ Meanwhile, heat a saucepan over medium heat. Using a pastry brush, coat the aubergine/eggplant slices with oil on both sides. Fry in the hot pan until golden brown on both sides and just tender. Transfer to a dish and give them a generous drizzle of oil. Season well with salt and pepper.

★ Layer the aubergine/eggplant slices in a casserole dish with the tomatoes, onions and basil leaves (reserving some for serving). Pour the cream over, drizzle over some oil and bake in the oven for 15–20 minutes until bubbling and golden on top.

★ Remove from the oven. Tear the remaining basil leaves and scatter over the top of the dish. Serve immediately.

MAC 'N' CHEESE with spinach

SOMETIMES YOU JUST NEED A CHEESY, FILLING HOT SIDE TO ACCOMPANY A BARBECUE PARTY OR COOKOUT, THIS WILL BE ESPECIALLY APPRECIATED AT NIGHT IF THE WEATHER IS A LITTLE COOLER. MAKING MAC 'N' CHEESE FROM SCRATCH IS NO BIG DEAL, AND IT TASTES SO MUCH BETTER THAN ANYTHING PRE-PREPARED YOU CAN BUY. THIS RECIPE HAS THE ADVANTAGE OF BUILT-IN VEGETABLES, SO THERE IS REALLY NO NEED FOR A SIDE SALAD...

50 g/3½ tablespoons butter

3 tablespoons plain/all-purpose flour

600 ml/2⅓ cups milk

100 g/1½ cups grated Cheddar, or more if liked

150 g/1 cup frozen spinach, defrosted

300 g/3 cups macaroni pasta

3–4 tablespoons wholemeal/ whole-wheat breadcrumbs

sea salt and freshly ground black pepper

a baking dish, generously buttered

makes 6–8 servings

★ Preheat the oven to 190°C (375°F) Gas 5.

★ Melt the butter in a saucepan set over medium heat. Add the flour and cook, stirring constantly with a wooden spoon, for 1 minute. Gradually add the milk, stirring continuously, and cook for about 5 minutes, until the sauce thickens. Season lightly, add the cheese and stir until melted. Remove from the heat and stir in the spinach. Taste and adjust the seasoning. Add more grated cheese, to taste.

★ Cook the macaroni according to the package instructions and drain. Put in the prepared dish and pour over the sauce. Mix well to combine and spread evenly. Sprinkle the breadcrumbs on top and bake in the preheated oven for 20–30 minutes, until bubbling. Serve hot.

Variation: Other vegetables such as leeks can be used in place of the spinach, and frozen defrosted vegetables work especially well here. Try sweet(corn) kernels, broccoli and cauliflower florets.

BBQ BREAD LOAF

THIS IS SUCH A FUN, RUSTIC RECIPE, IT MIGHT GET SLIGHTLY MESSY
WHEN SHARING OUT, BUT THAT IS PART OF THE JOY. MAKE SURE TO
SQUEEZE OUT THE EXCESS WATER PROPERLY FROM THE TOFU TO AVOID
A WATERY SAUCE. IF YOU DON'T HAVE A LARGE BREAD ROLL, MAKE THIS
WITH INDIVIDUAL SMALLER ONES INSTEAD.

1 onion, roughly chopped

1 red (bell) pepper, coarsely chopped

1 celery stick, chopped

2 tablespoons extra virgin olive oil or vegetable oil

2 garlic cloves, crushed

400 ml/1⅔ cups passata/strained tomatoes

2 teaspoons vegetarian Worcestershire sauce

1 teaspoon dried oregano

1 teaspoon ground cumin

1 tablespoon ketchup

1 tablespoon cider vinegar

1 generous tablespoon dark brown sugar

2 tablespoons barbecue sauce

400 g/14 oz. firm tofu, rinsed, drained, patted dry and cut into bite-size cubes

400-g/14-oz. bread loaf

sea salt and freshly ground black pepper

grated cheese, to serve

makes 4–6 servings

★ Put the onion, red (bell) pepper and celery in a food processor and blend until minced. Alternatively, chop very finely. Combine in a large frying pan/skillet with the oil and cook until soft, stirring often. Add the garlic and cook for 1 minute. Stir in the passata/strained tomatoes, Worcestershire sauce, oregano, cumin, ketchup, vinegar, sugar and barbecue sauce. Let simmer for 10 minutes. Taste and adjust the seasoning. Stir in the tofu and simmer, covered, for about 15–20 minutes more.

★ Meanwhile, slice the top off the loaf and set aside. Hollow out the loaf by pulling out the soft bread, shred and stir into the tofu mixture.

★ Preheat the oven to 200°C (400°F) Gas 6.

★ Set the bread loaf on a piece of kitchen foil large enough to wrap around the bread. Fill the hollow loaf with the tofu mixture and replace the bread lid. Enclose with the foil and bake in the preheated oven for 20 minutes.

★ Remove from the oven and serve warm, with grated cheese.

CHAPTER 5

SLAWS & SALADS

CLASSIC COLESLAW

----

125 g/1 generous cup shredded white cabbage

125 g/1 generous cup shredded red cabbage

175 g/1½ cups grated carrots

½ white onion, thinly sliced

1 teaspoon sea salt, plus extra for seasoning

2 teaspoons caster/superfine sugar

1 tablespoon white wine vinegar

50 ml/3½ tablespoons Classic Mayo (see page 116)

50 ml/3 tablespoons single/light cream

freshly ground black pepper

serves 4–6

★ Put the white and red cabbage, carrots and onion in a colander and sprinkle with the salt, sugar and vinegar. Stir well and let drain over a bowl for 20 minutes.

★ Transfer the vegetables to a clean kitchen cloth and squeeze out any excess liquid. Put them in a large bowl and stir in the mayo and cream. Season to taste with salt and pepper and serve.

SOUR CREAM SLAW

1 celery stick, grated

80 g/⅔ cup grated green cabbage

1 carrot, grated

½ red onion (or 3 spring onions/
scallions), finely chopped

1 teaspoon wholegrain mustard

1 tablespoon white wine vinegar

1 teaspoon dark brown sugar

100 ml/scant ½ cup sour cream

sea salt and freshly ground black
pepper

serves 4

BECAUSE OF ITS TANGY, FRESH TASTE, NOTHING GOES WITH WARM WEATHER LIKE HOMEMADE COLESLAW. IT'S A GREAT COMPONENT FOR A PARTY WITH FRIENDS OR A FAMILY GET-TOGETHER.

★ Put the celery, cabbage, carrot and onion in a large bowl. Stir in the mustard, white wine vinegar, sugar and sour cream. Season to taste with salt and pepper and serve.

ROSEMARY COLESLAW

HERBS AND SPICES ADD SURPRISING DEPTH OF FLAVOUR TO THIS
FRESH CRUNCHY COLESLAW – MAKING IT A CONDIMENT AND A
SALAD ALL AT ONCE. WHAT AN ALL-ROUND AMAZING DISH!

240 g/4 cups green or red cabbage,
sliced or shredded thinly

1 large carrot, roughly grated

¼ medium red onion, thinly sliced

1½ teaspoons sea salt, plus extra
for seasoning

dressing

60 g/¼ cup mayonnaise

60 g/¼ cup sour cream

1 teaspoon Dijon mustard

60 ml/¼ cup cider vinegar

¼ teaspoon caraway seeds

¼ teaspoon freshly ground black
pepper

1 teaspoon freshly chopped
rosemary

1 teaspoon caster/granulated sugar

1 small garlic clove, grated/minced

a pinch of cayenne pepper

serves 4

★ Place the cabbage, carrot and onion in a large colander set over a large
bowl or plate, sprinkle with salt and toss to coat. Place a heavy bowl on
top of the cabbage, then place a heavy can or two in the bowl to weigh it
down. Let it sit until the cabbage has released about 60 ml/¼ cup of
moisture, at least 1 hour.

★ Meanwhile, make the dressing. Add all the remaining ingredients, except
the sugar, pepper and salt to a large sterilized jar, screw the lid on securely
and shake. Add the sugar, pepper and salt to taste. Place the jar in the
refrigerator for 30–60 minutes.

★ Transfer the cabbage, carrot and onion to a medium-size bowl and pour
half the dressing over. Toss with tongs, cover and let the coleslaw sit for 30
minutes, tossing once or twice to redistribute the dressing. Toss once more
before serving and add additional dressing if desired. Leftover dressing will
keep for over 1 week in the refrigerator.

MANGO & LIME VEGETABLE SLAW

THIS ZINGY VEGETABLE SALAD MAKES A GREAT ACCOMPANIMENT TO LOTS OF SPICY DISHES. MANGOES AND LIMES ARE ESPECIALLY PROMINENT IN SOUTH INDIAN CUISINE AS WELL AS MOST ASIAN FOODS. SERVE THIS VIBRANT SLAW WITH ANY CURRY OR SPICY SNACK, OR AS PART OF A SOUTH INDIAN THALI PLATTER.

grated zest of 1 lime and freshly squeezed juice of 4 limes

250 ml/1 heaped cup mango pulp or purée

1 tablespoon tamari, or light soy sauce

¼ teaspoon salt, or to taste

1 teaspoon sugar (optional)

½ red cabbage, thinly sliced

½ white cabbage, thinly sliced

3 carrots, grated

a small handful of finely chopped fresh mint leaves (optional)

serves 4–6

★ Put the lime zest and juice in a large bowl. Add the mango pulp to the bowl with the tamari, salt and sugar, if using – omit if the mango purée is sweetened. Whisk together. Ensure the sugar is dissolved, then check the seasoning.

★ Add the shredded vegetables to the bowl, and stir the dressing through to ensure everything is well coated. Stir in the mint and serve.

BEET, CELERIAC/CELERY ROOT & APPLE REMOULADE

----

grated zest and juice of 1 lemon

5 tablespoons/⅓ cup Classic Mayo (see page 116)

2 apples, unpeeled, grated

¼ celeriac/celery root, peeled and grated

1 garlic clove, crushed

2 teaspoons fresh dill, finely chopped, plus a few extra sprigs, to serve

2 teaspoons Dijon mustard

1 teaspoon horseradish cream

2 small raw beet(roots), peeled and grated

a handful of chopped walnuts, to garnish

salt and freshly ground black pepper

goat's cheese toasts (optional)

1 crusty baguette

100 g/3½ oz. goat's cheese

a drizzle of olive oil

serves 4–6

THIS DELICIOUSLY CRUNCHY REMOULADE MAKES THE PERFECT SIDE DISH. IT'S ALSO IDEAL FOR A LIGHT LUNCH OR AS A SNACK, SHOWN HERE SERVED WITH CREAMY GOAT'S CHEESE TOASTS. YOU COULD ALSO TRY IT WITH THE HERBED TOASTS ON PAGE 15.

★ To make the remoulade, put the lemon zest and most of the juice in a small bowl with the mayonnaise. Add the remaining lemon juice to a bowl of cold water and put the apple and celeriac/celery root in the water to prevent them from discolouring.

★ Add the garlic, dill, mustard and horseradish cream to the mayonnaise and season to taste with salt and pepper. Drain the celeriac/celery root and apple and stir through the mayonnaise mixture, together with the grated beet(root).

★ To make the goat's cheese toasts, preheat the grill/broiler to hot. Cut the baguette into slices on an angle, spread one side with the goat's cheese, then drizzle with olive oil. Toast under the grill/broiler until warm and golden.

★ Spoon the remoulade into a serving bowl, scatter over some chopped walnuts and sprigs of dill and serve with the warm goat's cheese toasts.

TABBOULEH SALAD with feta

100 g/¾ cup bulgur wheat

250 g/9 oz. feta cheese, crumbled

2 shallots (or 1 small red onion), finely chopped

4 ripe tomatoes, chopped into 1-cm/½-inch pieces

2 bunches of fresh flat-leaf parsley, finely chopped

1 small bunch of fresh mint, finely chopped

3 tablespoons olive oil

freshly squeezed juice of 2 lemons, or more to taste, plus the grated zest of 1 lemon

sea salt and freshly ground black pepper

serves 6

SOMETIMES LESS IS MORE, AND THIS IS DEFINITELY THE CASE WITH THIS DIVINE DISH. MANY PEOPLE USE COUSCOUS INSTEAD OF THE TRADITIONAL BULGUR WHEAT BUT THE REAL STAR OF THE SHOW IS, AND SHOULD BE, THE PARSLEY.

★ Put the bulgur wheat in a shallow bowl and pour over enough cold water to cover. Leave for 20 minutes or so for the wheat to soften, then transfer to a sieve/strainer and rinse the wheat under cold water until the water runs clear and all the starch is removed. Drain well.

★ Put the wheat in a large mixing bowl and mix well with a fork to separate any grains. Throw in the feta, chopped shallot, tomatoes (and any tomato juices released when chopping) and herbs and season well with salt and pepper.

★ In a separate small bowl, whisk together the olive oil and the lemon juice and zest. Taste this and add more lemon juice if it is not tart enough. Gently pour the dressing over the tabbouleh and mix really well.

QUINOA SALAD with spring vegetables

DUE TO ITS INCREDIBLE HEALTH BENEFITS AND PLEASING TEXTURE, QUINOA SHOULD REALLY BE JUST AS POPULAR AS RICE OR PASTA FOR YOUR DAILY COOKING NEEDS, IF NOT MORE SO. THIS TASTY SALAD IS A CELEBRATION OF NEW-SEASON SPRING VEGETABLES.

300 g/1½ cups quinoa

2 teaspoons stock/bouillon powder

12 asparagus spears, sliced in half

200 g/2 cups shelled broad/fava beans

200 g/2 cups peas

a large handful of fresh mint leaves

a handful of fresh flat-leaf parsley

a handful of cherry tomatoes, halved

grated zest and juice of 1 lemon

200 ml/1⅓ cups extra virgin olive oil

2 tablespoons agave syrup

1 tablespoon pomegranate molasses (or balsamic vinegar)

sea salt and freshly ground black pepper

serves 6

★ Put the quinoa and stock/bouillon powder in a saucepan and cover with just under double its volume of water. Bring to the boil, then reduce the heat to low and place the lid on top. Cook for about 12 minutes until all the water has been absorbed. Turn off the heat, remove the lid and let any remaining water evaporate. Remove to a wide plate or tray and let cool.

★ Meanwhile, bring a pan of water to the boil (just enough to cover each set of vegetables you are cooking) and add 2 teaspoons salt. Cook the asparagus, beans and peas separately until just tender – about 3–4 minutes for each. You still want them to have a bit of bite.

★ Once the beans are cooked, they need to have their outer cases removed. This is time consuming but the end result is truly worth it, for the colour if for nothing else. Simply slide the pale case off each bean and discard.

★ Roughly chop the herbs. In a large bowl, gently but thoroughly mix the quinoa, asparagus, beans, peas, tomatoes and herbs, reserving some of the herbs for serving. Add the lemon zest and juice, oil, agave syrup, molasses, salt and pepper. Mix again, taste and adjust the seasoning if necessary.

★ Serve in a large dish with the remaining herbs sprinkled on top. Finish off with a drizzle of oil.

SALAD OF SOY, WHEAT BERRIES & CASHEWS

200 g/1⅓ cups wheat berries

750 ml/3 cups boiling salted water

1 tablespoon dark soy sauce

1 tablespoon vegetarian oyster sauce

4 spring onions/scallions, finely chopped

30 g/3 tablespoons roasted cashew nuts

serves 4–6

WHEAT BERRIES ARE A NEWCOMER ON THE SUPERFOOD STREET CORNER. IF YOU HAVE NOT HEARD OF THEM, KEEP A LOOK OUT IN THE SPECIAL SELECTION FOOD AISLE OF YOUR SUPERMARKET/STORE. OTHERWISE, THEY ARE EASY TO FIND ONLINE. SLIGHTLY DIFFERENT FROM BARLEY OR PUFFED WHEAT, THEY HAVE A FIRM AND SUPPLE TEXTURE AND HOLD THEIR OWN WITH THE SOY SAUCE. THE SWEET ROASTED CASHEW NUTS ADD TEXTURE AND CRUNCH.

★ Put the wheat berries and boiling salted water in a saucepan and cook uncovered over low heat for about 45 minutes, or until the berries are soft. Drain well.

★ In a large bowl, combine the warm wheat berries, soy sauce, vegetarian oyster sauce and spring onions/scallions and allow to sit for at least 30 minutes so that the wheat berries can absorb the sauce. (You can make this the day before and refrigerate it once the wheat berries have cooled to room temperature.)

★ Finally, stir through the cashew nuts just before serving so that they keep their crunch.

BASIL, MOZZARELLA & ORZO SALAD

ITALIANS KNOW A THING OR TWO ABOUT FLAVOUR COMBINATIONS. THIS DISH IS FULL OF RUSTIC CHARM AND DELICIOUS AUTHENTIC INGREDIENTS. SERVE ALONGSIDE A MEDITERRANEAN-STYLE BARBECUE/GRILL SPREAD IN THE SUNSHINE WITH A LARGE GLASS OF WHITE WINE ON THE SIDE.

a large handful of fresh basil, roughly chopped

20 g/¼ cup finely grated Italian-style hard cheese

1 garlic clove

25 g/3 tablespoons toasted pine nuts/kernels, plus a few extra to garnish

1 tablespoon extra virgin olive oil

175 g/1 cup orzo pasta

150 g/5½ oz. mozzarella, torn

50 g/⅓ cup sun-blushed (semi-dried) tomatoes, roughly chopped

a handful of wild rocket/arugula

sea salt and freshly ground black pepper

serves 2

★ In a food processor, whizz up most of the basil (keep a few leaves back for garnish), the grated Italian-style hard cheese, garlic, pine nuts/kernels, olive oil and a grind of salt and pepper to make a fresh pesto dressing.

★ Bring a small pan of water to the boil, add the orzo and cook for 8 minutes or until al dente. Drain and refresh under cold running water before draining again.

★ In a large mixing bowl, combine the orzo and the pesto dressing, mixing thoroughly, then add the torn mozzarella, chopped tomatoes and rocket/arugula and toss through. Lastly, garnish with a few sprigs of basil and a sprinkling of pine nuts/kernels before serving.

LEMON, GARLIC & CHILLI/ CHILE POTATO SALAD

THE POTATO SALAD IS ONE OF THOSE ALL-TIME FAVOURITES AT ANY OUTDOOR EATING EVENT. THIS VERSION IS NO EXCEPTION, HOWEVER IT DOES DIFFER A LITTLE FROM THE ORIGINAL MAYONNAISE VERSION. THE FLAVOURS USED ARE LIGHTER AND BRIGHTER. THE CHILLI/CHILE PACKS A PUNCH WITH HEAT WHILE THE COOLING LEMON AND HERBS MINGLE WITH THE GARLIC BUTTER.

1 kg/2¼ lb. new potatoes, unpeeled

100 g/6½ tablespoons butter, softened

2 garlic cloves, crushed

freshly squeezed juice and grated zest of 2 lemons

1 long green chilli/chile, finely diced

a small handful of fresh flat-leaf parsley, roughly chopped

a small handful of fresh chives, roughly chopped

sea salt and freshly ground black pepper

serves 6

★ Thoroughly wash the new potatoes under cold running water to remove any dirt, then put them in a large saucepan of lightly salted water and bring to the boil. Cook for about 15–20 minutes, until the potatoes are just tender when pierced with a knife.

★ While the potatoes are cooking, put the butter, garlic, lemon juice and chilli/chile in a small bowl and mix well.

★ Drain the potatoes and transfer them to a large mixing bowl, halving and quartering them as you go. Add the butter mixture to the bowl while the potatoes are still warm and gently stir to coat the potatoes. When the potatoes have cooled, sprinkle over the lemon zest and fresh herbs, season with salt and a little pepper and mix well again to thoroughly combine.

NEW POTATO SALAD
with gazpacho dressing

GAZPACHO IS THE FAMOUS SPANISH CHILLED SOUP, MADE WITH TOMATOES, (BELL) PEPPERS, ONIONS AND GARLIC. USE THE SAME INGREDIENTS TO MAKE A FRESH DRESSING FOR THIS SIMPLE SALAD OF NEW POTATOES. ADD THE DRESSING TO THE POTATOES WHILE THEY ARE HOT, EVEN IF YOU AREN'T EATING THEM STRAIGHT AWAY, AS THIS WILL HELP THE FLAVOURS TO INFUSE.

★ Thoroughly wash the new potatoes under cold running water to remove any dirt, then put them in a large saucepan of lightly salted water and bring to the boil. Cook for about 10–15 minutes, until the potatoes are just tender when pierced with a knife.

★ Meanwhile, put all the dressing ingredients in a large bowl and mix well. Add plenty of salt and pepper.

★ Drain the potatoes thoroughly. Add them to the dressing and toss well. Serve hot or let cool to room temperature.

500 g/18 oz. new potatoes, unpeeled

dressing

2 large, ripe tomatoes, halved, deseeded and diced

50 g/2 oz. preserved roasted red (bell) peppers (from a jar), diced

½ small red onion, chopped

1 garlic clove, chopped

3 tablespoons extra virgin olive oil

2 teaspoons red wine vinegar

a pinch of sugar

a bunch of fresh flat-leaf parsley, roughly chopped

sea salt and freshly ground black pepper

serves 4

COURGETTE/ZUCCHINI & FETA SALAD

with lemon, caper & mint dressing

---

4 large courgettes/zucchini

¼ teaspoon dried red chilli/
hot pepper flakes

1 tablespoon extra virgin olive oil

200 g/7 oz. feta, sliced and crumbled
into fairly large pieces

4 tablespoons toasted pine nuts/
kernels

sea salt and freshly ground black
pepper

dressing

4 tablespoons extra virgin olive oil

1 tablespoon freshly squeezed lemon
juice

½ teaspoon balsamic vinegar, plus
extra to taste

½ teaspoon grated lemon zest

1–2 garlic cloves, finely chopped

1 tablespoon freshly chopped mint,
plus a few whole leaves to garnish

2 tablespoons freshly chopped
flat-leaf parsley

2 tablespoons small salted capers,
rinsed and soaked in cold water for
10 minutes, then drained

serves 4–6

THIS DISH MAKES A LOVELY FIRST COURSE, EITHER ALONE OR AS PART OF A MIXED ANTIPASTI WITH SOME GRILLED (BELL) PEPPERS, BOTTLED ARTICHOKES OR A GRILLED AUBERGINE/EGGPLANT DIP. ALTERNATIVELY, SERVE IT AS AN ACCOMPANIMENT TO YOUR BARBECUE/GRILL FEAST.

★ Cut the courgettes/zucchini lengthways into slices. Put in a colander and toss with 1 teaspoon salt. Leave for 30–60 minutes to drain in the sink, then rinse and dry on paper towels.

★ Season with lots of pepper and the chilli flakes/hot pepper flakes, if using. Add the oil and toss to coat.

★ Preheat the barbecue/grill. Once it is hot, cook the courgettes/zucchini for 6–8 minutes, turning once, until lightly charred and just tender. Put the courgettes/zucchini in a dish to cool.

★ To make the dressing, put the oil, lemon juice, balsamic vinegar, lemon zest, garlic and chopped mint and parsley in a bowl and whisk well. Stir in the capers and pour the dressing over the courgettes/zucchini. Cover and set aside for 30–60 minutes for the flavours to marry. Just before serving, mix in the feta and serve sprinkled with the pine nuts/kernels and a few mint leaves.

½ red onion, sliced

6 red (bell) peppers

450 g/1 lb. asparagus, trimmed

extra virgin olive oil, for brushing

200 g/1¼ cups mangetout/snowpeas

100 g/3½ oz. mixed salad leaves

a handful each of fresh flat-leaf parsley and dill

60 g/¾ cup hazelnuts, toasted and roughly chopped

dressing

60 ml/¼ cup hazelnut oil

2 tablespoons extra virgin olive oil

1 tablespoon sherry vinegar

1 teaspoon caster/superfine sugar

sea salt and freshly ground black pepper

serves 4–6

ROASTED RED BELL PEPPER & ASPARAGUS SALAD

VEGETABLES TASTE WONDERFUL WHEN COOKED ON THE BARBECUE OR GRILL – IT BRINGS OUT THEIR NATURAL SWEETNESS. THIS SALAD WILL SERVE FOUR AS AN ENTRÉE OR SIX AS AN APPETIZER.

★ Put the onion slices in a strainer, sprinkle with salt and leave to drain over a bowl for 30 minutes. Rinse the onion under cold running water and pat dry with paper towels.

★ Preheat the barbecue/grill. Once it is hot, cook the (bell) peppers for 15 minutes, turning frequently until charred all over. Transfer to a plastic bag, seal and let soften until cool. Peel off the skin and discard the seeds, then cut the flesh into thick strips.

★ Brush the asparagus with olive oil and cook on the hot barbecue/grill for 3–4 minutes, turning frequently, until charred and tender.

★ Put the mangetout/snowpeas in a saucepan of lightly salted boiling water and cook for 1–2 minutes. Drain and refresh under cold water.

★ Put the onion, (bell) peppers, asparagus, and mangetout/snowpeas in a bowl and toss gently. Add the salad leaves, herbs, and hazelnuts. Put all the dressing ingredients in a bowl and beat well. Season to taste with salt and pepper, then pour over the salad and toss to coat. Serve immediately.

POMEGRANATE & SQUASH
SALAD with a balsamic dressing

1 large butternut squash

a drizzle of olive oil

1 tablespoon crushed dried red chilli/hot pepper flakes (optional)

2 tablespoons coriander seeds

2 tablespoons cumin seeds

200 g/7 oz. rocket/arugula leaves, washed and dried

seeds from 1 large pomegranate (save the juice) or 150 g/5½ oz. pre-packed pomegranate seeds

a handful of fresh mint leaves

sea salt and freshly ground black pepper

dressing

2 tablespoons balsamic vinegar

freshly squeezed juice of ½ lemon

1 tablespoon pomegranate molasses (or leftover pomegranate juice if you cannot find)

3 tablespoons olive oil

sea salt and freshly ground black pepper

serves 6

SIMPLE INGREDIENTS THAT PACK A PUNCH WITH FLAVOUR, THAT IS WHAT THIS SALAD IS ALL ABOUT. THE SWEETNESS OF BUTTERNUT SQUASH WORKS WELL WITH THE HEAT FROM THE CHILLI/CHILE AND SPICES, BUT PUMPKIN OR ROASTED SWEET POTATOES WOULD ALSO WORK WELL. YOU CAN BUY PRE-PACKED POMEGRANATE SEEDS FROM MANY SUPERMARKETS/STORES IN THE FRUIT AND VEGETABLE AISLE, BUT IF YOU HAVE TO EXTRACT THEM FROM THE FRUIT YOURSELF, THE JUICE THAT RUNS OUT MAKES A LOVELY ADDITION TO THE DRESSING.

★ Preheat the oven to 200°C (400°F) Gas 6.

★ Slice the butternut squash in half lengthways and discard all the seeds and stringy bits (leave the skin on). Slice the halves into long strips about 1 cm/ ½ inch thick. Arrange these on a baking sheet.

★ In a pestle and mortar, roughly grind the red chilli/hot pepper flakes and spice seeds together, then sprinkle them evenly over the butternut squash. Drizzle a really good glug of olive oil over and season well with salt and pepper. Pop in the preheated oven and roast for about 25–30 minutes, until the edges are just browning and the squash is tender and cooked but not dried out. Leave to cool.

★ Toss the rocket/arugula leaves, pomegranate seeds and mint leaves together. Transfer to a serving dish and arrange the squash on top.

★ To make the balsamic dressing, combine all the ingredients together in a jar and shake well to mix. Drizzle over the salad just before serving.

GRILLED PITTA SALAD
with olive salsa & mozzarella

FATOUSH IS A BREAD SALAD MADE FROM GRILLED PITTA BREAD. IT'S OFTEN ACCOMPANIED BY HALLOUMI, A FIRM CHEESE THAT CAN BE CHARGRILLED. FRESH MOZZARELLA CHEESE CAN ALSO BE COOKED ON THE GRILL. IT PICKS UP AN APPEALING SMOKINESS IN THE PROCESS.

225 g/8 oz. fresh mozzarella, drained

1 large green (bell) pepper, deseeded and diced

1 small cucumber, diced

2 ripe tomatoes, chopped

½ red onion, finely chopped

2 pitta breads

60 ml/¼ cup extra virgin olive oil

freshly squeezed juice of ½ lemon

sea salt and freshly ground black pepper

salsa

75 g/3 oz. Kalamata olives, pitted and chopped

1 tablespoon freshly chopped flat-leaf parsley

1 small garlic clove, finely chopped

60 ml/¼ cup extra virgin olive oil

1 tablespoon freshly squeezed lemon juice

serves 4

★ Preheat the barbecue/grill.

★ Wrap the mozzarella in paper towels and squeeze to remove excess water. Unwrap and cut into thick slices. Brush the slices well with olive oil. Cook on the hot barbecue/grill for 1 minute on each side until the cheese is charred with lines and beginning to soften. Alternatively, simply slice the cheese and use without grilling.

★ Put the green (bell) pepper, cucumber, tomatoes and onion in a bowl. Toast the pitta breads on the barbecue/grill. Let cool slightly, then tear into bite-size pieces. Add to the bowl, then pour over 1–2 tablespoons olive oil and a little lemon juice. Season with salt and pepper and stir.

★ Put all the ingredients for the salsa in a bowl and stir well.

★ Spoon the salad onto plates, top with a few slices of mozzarella and some olive salsa, and serve.

750 g/1½ lb. new potatoes or baby potatoes, unpeeled

220 g/8 oz. French beans

1–2 tablespoons caper berries, drained

a handful of fresh tarragon leaves, roughly chopped

2 small preserved black summer truffles (optional)

sea salt and freshly ground black pepper

dressing

1 tablespoon white wine vinegar

1 tablespoon olive oil

1 teaspoon wholegrain mustard

2–3 teaspoons truffle oil

serves 6

SALAD OF TRUFFLED FRENCH BEANS

ONE OF THE MOST LUXURIOUS INGREDIENTS IN LIFE IS THE TRUFFLE FUNGUS. A TRUFFLE HAS ONE OF THOSE DELICIOUS SUBTLE QUALITIES THAT CAN REALLY ENHANCE A DISH. ADDING A DECADENT TRUFFLE TO A RUSTIC SALAD OF POTATOES AND GREEN BEANS IS ONE WAY TO SHOWCASE THE SUBLIME MORSEL. PRESERVED TRUFFLES CAN BE FOUND IN THE SPECIALIST INGREDIENTS AISLE OF A SUPERMARKET/ STORE OR IN FINE FOODS DELICATESSENS.

★ Bring the potatoes to the boil in a saucepan of salted water. After simmering for 8 minutes, add a steamer above the saucepan with the French beans and cook both the potatoes and beans for a further 3 minutes. (The potatoes should have a total of 10–11 minutes until they are cooked through.) Drain and refresh both the potatoes and beans under cold running water until completely cool, then dry off.

★ For the dressing, put the vinegar and olive oil in a jar or other sealable container, add a generous pinch of salt, the wholegrain mustard, black pepper and finish with the truffle oil, then shake together.

★ Toss together the beans and potatoes with the caper berries and tarragon. If you managed to find black summer truffles, use a vegetable or truffle peeler to shave very thin slices over the salad and toss through. Season the salad with sea salt and black pepper and finally drizzle with truffle dressing just before serving.

CARROT, BLOOD ORANGE & WALNUT SALAD

2 blood oranges

8 large carrots, grated

grated zest and juice of 1 lemon

3 tablespoons agave syrup

1 tablespoon freshly chopped flat-leaf parsley

4 tablespoons extra virgin olive oil

sea salt

2 handfuls of walnuts, fresh from the shell

serves 6

THE COLOUR OF THIS BLOOD ORANGE SALAD IS ENOUGH TO WIN ANYONE OVER, BUT IT IS FULL OF FLAVOUR AS WELL. IT'S PERFECT AS A SIDE OR PARTNERED WITH A NUMBER OF OTHER SALADS, ALL SUMPTUOUSLY LAID OUT TOGETHER. MAKE SURE YOU GET YOUR HANDS ON BLOOD ORANGES WHILE THEY ARE IN SEASON.

★ Cut the top and bottom off the oranges, just down to the flesh, then place the orange on its end, cut side down, and carefully, following the shape of the orange, cut the peel off in strips from top to bottom, making sure you cut off the white pith too. Then turn them on their side and cut them into 1-cm/½-inch thick rounds. Do this on a board or somewhere that will catch any orange juice that you inadvertently squeeze out of them; this can be added to the dish too.

★ Squeeze any excess juice out of the grated carrots to prevent the salad from being too soggy (you can drink any juice you extract). In a large bowl, combine the carrots with all the other ingredients. This should be a punchy, citrussy salad with just enough sweetness from the agave. Let all the flavours combine together for a few minutes, then taste again, adjust the seasoning with more juice, parsley, salt and agave if necessary.

CHICORY/ENDIVE LEAVES STUFFED WITH BEET, CUMIN & MIXED GRAINS

50 g/heaped ¼ cup basmati rice

5 cardamom pods

50 g/heaped ¼ cup quinoa

2 teaspoons cumin seeds

2 teaspoons fennel seeds

100 g/¾ cup canned chickpeas, strained and rinsed well

grated zest and freshly squeezed juice of 2 limes

a small handful of fresh coriander/cilantro leaves, finely chopped, plus extra to serve

½ raw beet(root), peeled and grated (gloves are advisable as beet(root) dyes your hands)

70 g/½ cup pistachios, whole or roughly chopped, plus extra to serve

2 tablespoons groundnut/peanut oil (or olive oil, rapeseed/canola oil all work well)

a pinch of caster/superfine sugar

15 middle-outer chicory/endive leaves, washed and dried

salt and freshly ground black pepper

makes 15

THIS TASTY SALAD MAKES A GREAT ADDITION TO ANY BUFFET. THE CHICORY/ENDIVE LEAF GIVES A BITTER EDGE TO CUT THROUGH THE SWEETNESS OF THE BEET(ROOT). YOU CAN PREPARE IT IN ADVANCE, BUT HOLD BACK SOME GARNISHES AS THE BEETS COLOUR EVERYTHING.

★ Wash the rice well and put it in a large saucepan with boiling salted water and the cardamom pods. Cook according to the packet instructions until soft but still with a bite. Strain well, spread on a tray to cool down and set aside.

★ Meanwhile, cook the quinoa in boiling salted water – just enough to cover the grains by 5 mm/¼ inch. Gently simmer for about 10 minutes, until softened but retaining a bite. Strain well, spread on a tray to cool down and set aside.

★ Lightly toast the cumin and fennel seeds in a dry frying pan/skillet set over medium heat – just until you can smell the aromas of the seeds releasing – then turn off the heat, remove from the pan and set aside.

★ In a bowl, combine the chickpeas, rice, quinoa, lime zest, coriander/cilantro, cumin and fennel seeds, beet(root), pistachios, salt and pepper, and mix well. Taste the mixture and season with the oil, lime juice, sugar, salt and pepper. Once seasoned, fill the chicory/endive leaves generously and sprinkle with the freshly chopped coriander/cilantro and the remaining pistachios.

CHAPTER 6

SAUCES, SALSAS & RUBS

HOT & SMOKY BARBECUE SAUCE

HOMEMADE SAUCES ARE TASTY AND SIMPLE TO MAKE. THEY WILL STORE WELL FOR UP TO 5 DAYS OR FOR SEVERAL WEEKS IN STERILIZED JARS IN THE FRIDGE.

★ Put all the ingredients in a saucepan, bring to the boil and simmer gently for 15 minutes until thickened and reduced. Season to taste with salt and pepper, then let cool completely.

★ Pour into a clean jar and store in the fridge for up to five days. If using sterilized jars, pour the hot sauce directly into the jar and when cold, seal and store in the fridge. It will keep for a few weeks.

200 ml/¾ cup passata/strained tomatoes

100 ml/scant ½ cup maple syrup

50 ml/3 tablespoons black treacle/dark molasses

50 ml/3 tablespoons tomato ketchup, homemade (see right) or store bought

50 ml/3 tablespoons white wine vinegar

2 tablespoons vegetarian Worcestershire sauce

1 tablespoon hot chilli/chile sauce

2 teaspoons Dijon mustard

1 teaspoon garlic powder

1 teaspoon smoked paprika

sea salt and freshly ground black pepper

makes 350 ml/1½ cups

HOMEMADE TOMATO KETCHUP

GIVE THE STEADFAST KETCHUP FANS IN YOUR LIFE A REAL TREAT WITH THIS
EASY RECIPE, IT IS SO MUCH BETTER THAN THE STORE-BOUGHT VERSION.

2 tablespoons olive oil

1 onion, finely chopped

2 garlic cloves, crushed

450 ml/2 scant cups passata/
strained tomatoes

150 ml/⅔ cup red wine vinegar

150 g/¾ cup soft brown sugar

2 tablespoons black treacle/
dark molasses

2 tablespoons tomato purée/paste

1 teaspoon Dijon mustard

2 bay leaves

1 teaspoon sea salt

½ teaspoon freshly ground black
pepper

makes about 400 ml/1¾ cups

★ Heat the oil in a saucepan, add the
onion and garlic and fry gently for
10 minutes until softened.

★ Add the remaining ingredients, bring
to the boil, reduce the heat and simmer
gently for 30 minutes until thickened
and reduced by about one third.

★ Pass the sauce through a sieve/
strainer, let cool and pour into a clean
bottle and store in the fridge for up to
five days. If using sterilized bottles, pour
the hot sauce directly into the bottle
and when cold, seal and store in the
fridge. It will keep for a few weeks.

SWEET CHILLI/CHILE SAUCE

SWEET CHILLI SAUCE GOES BEAUTIFULLY WITH ALMOST ANYTHING, FROM SALADS AND GRILLED VEGETABLES TO SALTY HALLOUMI BURGERS. YOU NAME IT, IT TASTES GREAT WITH IT!

6 large red chillies/chiles, deseeded and chopped
4 garlic cloves, chopped
1 teaspoon grated/minced root ginger
1 teaspoon salt
100 ml/⅓ cup rice wine vinegar
100 g/½ cup caster/superfine sugar

makes about 200 ml/generous ¾ cup

★ Put the chillies/chiles, garlic, ginger and salt in a food processor and blend to a coarse paste. Transfer to a saucepan, add the vinegar and sugar, bring to the boil and simmer gently, part-covered, for 5 minutes until the mixture becomes a thin syrup. Remove from the heat and let cool.

★ Pour into an airtight container and store in the refrigerator for up to 2 weeks.

ASIAN BARBECUE SAUCE

FOR SOMETHING A LITTLE DIFFERENT ON THE SIDE, GIVE THIS FRAGRANT BARBECUE SAUCE A TRY. YOU COULD ALSO USE IT TO MARINATE CUBES OF TOFU READY FOR SKEWERING AND GRILLING.

100 ml/⅓ cup passata/strained tomatoes
50 ml/3½ tablespoons hoisin sauce
1 teaspoon hot chilli/chile sauce
2 garlic cloves, crushed
2 tablespoons sweet soy sauce
1 tablespoon rice wine vinegar
1 teaspoon ground coriander
½ teaspoon ground cinnamon
¼ teaspoon Chinese five-spice powder

makes about 350 ml/1½ cups

★ Put all the ingredients into a small saucepan, add 100 ml/⅓ cup water, bring to the boil and simmer gently for 10 minutes. Remove the pan from the heat and let cool.

★ Pour into an airtight container and store in the refrigerator for up to 2 weeks.

CLASSIC MAYO

3 egg yolks

2 teaspoons Dijon mustard

2 teaspoons white wine vinegar or freshly squeezed lemon juice

½ teaspoon sea salt

300 ml/2 cups olive oil

makes about 400 ml/2 cups

★ Put the egg yolks, mustard, vinegar or lemon juice and salt in a food processor and blend until foaming. With the blade running, gradually pour in the oil through a funnel until thick and glossy. If it is too thick add a little water. Adjust the seasoning to taste.

★ Spoon into a bowl and serve. Keeps well in the refrigerator for up to three days.

MUSTARD MAYO

1 recipe Classic Mayo

2 tablespoons wholegrain mustard

makes about 400 ml/2 cups

★ Make the Classic Mayo following the method in the recipe, left, but omitting the Dijon mustard. Transfer to a bowl and stir in the wholegrain mustard. Use as required or store as before in the refrigerator.

HERB MAYO

- - - - - - - - - - - - - - - - -

1 recipe Classic Mayo

a handful of any freshly chopped green herbs, such as basil, parsley or tarragon

makes about 400 ml/2 cups

★ Make the Classic Mayo following the method in the recipe, far left. Add the herbs to the food processor and blend until the sauce is speckled green. Use as required or store as before.

LEMON MAYO

- - - - - - - - - - - - - - - - -

1 recipe Classic Mayo

1 teaspoon freshly squeezed lemon juice

1 teaspoon finely grated lemon zest

a pinch of freshly ground black pepper

makes about 400 ml/2 cups

★ Make the Classic Mayo following the method in the recipe, far left, adding the lemon juice, zest and pepper with the mustard and vinegar. Blend until thickened. Use as required or store as before.

Variation: For a Lime Mayo, simply replace the lemon zest and juice with the zest and juice from a lime.

PESTO MAYO

- - - - - - - - - - - - - - - - -

1 recipe Classic Mayo

1 teaspoon fresh green pesto

makes about 400 ml/2 cups

★ Make the Classic Mayo following the method in the recipe, far left, adding the pesto at the same time as the mustard and vinegar. Blend until thickened. Use as required or store as before.

THAI SPICED MARINADE

2 lemongrass stalks

6 kaffir lime leaves

2 garlic cloves, roughly chopped

2.5-cm/1-inch piece of root ginger, peeled and finely chopped

4 coriander/cilantro roots, washed and dried

2 small fresh red chillies/chiles, deseeded and roughly chopped

200 ml/1⅓ cups extra virgin olive oil

2 tablespoons sesame oil

2 tablespoons soy sauce

makes about 300 ml/2 cups

★ Using a sharp knife, trim the lemongrass stalks down to 15 cm/ 6 inches, then remove and discard the tough outer layers. Chop the inner stalks coarsely.

★ Put the lemongrass stalks, lime leaves, garlic, ginger, coriander/ cilantro roots and chillies/chiles in a mortar and pound with a pestle to release the aromas.

★ Transfer the mixture to a bowl, add the oils and soy sauce and set aside to infuse until you are ready to marinate.

MINTED YOGURT MARINADE

2 teaspoons coriander seeds

1 teaspoon cumin seeds

250 ml/1¼ cups thick yogurt

freshly squeezed juice of ½ lemon

1 tablespoon extra virgin olive oil

2 garlic cloves, crushed

1 teaspoon grated/minced root ginger

½ teaspoon salt

2 tablespoons freshly chopped mint leaves

¼ teaspoon chilli/chili powder

makes about 275 ml/1½ cups

★ Put the coriander and cumin seeds in a dry frying pan/skillet and toast over medium heat until golden and aromatic. Remove from the heat and let cool. Transfer to a spice grinder and crush to a coarse powder. Alternatively, use a mortar and pestle.

★ Put the spices in a bowl, add the yogurt, lemon juice, olive oil, garlic, ginger, salt, mint and chilli/chili powder and mix well. Set aside to infuse until ready to use.

HERB, LEMON & GARLIC MARINADE

2 sprigs of fresh rosemary

2 sprigs of fresh thyme

4 bay leaves

2 large garlic cloves, roughly chopped

pared zest of 1 lemon

1 teaspoon black peppercorns, coarsely crushed

200 ml/1⅓ cups extra virgin olive oil

makes about 300 ml/2 cups

★ Strip the rosemary and thyme leaves from their stalks and put in a mortar. Add the bay leaves, garlic and lemon zest. Pound with a pestle to release the aroma of the ingredients.

★ Put the mixture in a bowl and add the peppercorns and olive oil. Set aside to infuse until you are ready to marinate.

BLUE CHEESE DRESSING

A CLASSIC DRESSING FOR WEDGES OF CHILLED COS OR ICEBERG LETTUCE – YOU CAN EXPERIMENT WITH DIFFERENT TYPES OF BLUE CHEESE TO GIVE YOU THE FLAVOUR THAT WORKS BEST. SOME BLUE CHEESES LIKE GORGONZOLA AND ROQUEFORT ARE NOT SUITABLE FOR VEGETARIANS, BUT SAINT AGUR AND DOLCELATTE ARE BOTH PARTICULARLY GOOD ALTERNATIVES, IT'S REALLY UP TO YOU.

75 ml/⅓ cup sour cream

50 g/¼ cup creamy blue cheese

1 tablespoon white wine vinegar

2 teaspoons just-boiled water

2 tablespoons extra virgin olive oil

1 tablespoon freshly chopped chives

salt and freshly ground black pepper

makes about 200 ml/1 cup

★ Place the sour cream, cheese, vinegar, water and a little salt and pepper in a food processor and blend until fairly smooth. Add the oil and blend again. Stir in the chives, adjust seasoning to taste and serve.

★ This creamy dressing, with its lovely tang of acidity from the blue cheese, is wonderful with cos or iceberg lettuce. It also works well with all green leaf salads, celery, apple, pear and mixed nuts.

SMOKY TOMATO SALSA

----

4 ripe plum tomatoes

2 large red chillies/chiles

4 garlic cloves, peeled

1 red onion, quartered

4 tablespoons extra virgin olive oil

1 tablespoon freshly squeezed lemon juice

2 tablespoons freshly chopped coriander/cilantro

sea salt and freshly ground black pepper

2 wooden skewers, soaked in water for 30 minutes

serves 4–6

★ Preheat the barbecue/grill.

★ Using tongs, hold the tomatoes over the flames of the barbecue/grill for about 1 minute, turning frequently, until the skin is charred all over. Let cool, peel, cut in half and deseed, then chop the flesh. Repeat with the chillies/chiles.

★ Thread the garlic cloves and onion wedges onto separate skewers. Cook the garlic over the hot barbecue/grill for 5–6 minutes and the onion for 10–12 minutes, turning frequently, until charred and softened. Let cool, remove from the skewers and dice into cubes.

★ Put the tomato, chillies/chiles, garlic and onion in a bowl and stir in the oil, lemon juice and coriander/cilantro. Season to taste with salt and pepper and use as required, or spoon into sterilized jars and store in the refrigerator for up to 3 days.

SALSA VERDE

- - - - - - - - - - - - - -

a large handful of flat-leaf parsley

a small bunch of mixed fresh herbs such as basil, chives and mint

1 garlic clove, chopped

1 tablespoon pitted green olives

1 tablespoon capers, drained and rinsed

1 teaspoon Dijon mustard

2 teaspoons white wine vinegar

150 ml/1 cup extra virgin olive oil

sea salt and freshly ground black pepper

serves 4

★ Put all the ingredients except the oil in a food processor and blend to a smooth paste. Gradually pour in the oil to form a sauce, then taste and adjust the seasoning. The salsa may be stored in the refrigerator for up to 3 days.

MANGO & SESAME SALSA

1 large ripe mango

4 spring onions/scallions, trimmed and finely chopped

1 small red chilli/chile, deseeded and chopped

1 garlic clove, crushed

1 tablespoon light soy sauce

1 tablespoon lime juice

1 teaspoon sesame oil

½ tablespoon caster/superfine sugar

1 tablespoon freshly chopped coriander/cilantro

sea salt and freshly ground black pepper

serves 4

★ Peel the mango and cut the flesh away from the pit. Cut the flesh into cubes and mix with all the remaining ingredients and season to taste. Set aside for 30 minutes for the flavours to infuse before serving.

HOME-FERMENTED KIMCHI

THIS IS JUST ONE OF MANY VARIATIONS OF KIMCHI, THE KOREAN DELICACY OF FERMENTED CABBAGE. AS WELL AS BEING DELICIOUS, HOME-FERMENTED FOODS ARE GREAT FOR DIGESTION AND AS SUCH ARE CURRENTLY ENJOYING A REVIVAL AMONGST COOKS. PILE THE SOUR, SALTY AND SPICY PICKLED CABBAGE ONTO BURGERS OR SERVE AS A FLAVOURSOME SIDE DISH. IT IS WORTH MAKING PLENTY AT ONCE AND USING IT UP IN 30–60 DAYS.

1.2 litres/5 cups water

3 tablespoons sea salt

600 g/7 cups julienned green cabbage

180 g/2½ cups leeks, chopped

20 g/¾ oz. piece of root ginger, peeled

4 garlic cloves, peeled

10 g/1 handful of dulse seaweed

1 teaspoon ground turmeric

1 whole medium-size green chilli/chile

a pickle press, optional

makes 12–15 servings

★ Make a brine by mixing the water and salt and stirring well until the salt dissolves. Put the cabbage and leeks into a pickle press and cover with the brine. To keep them submerged, screw the lid down just a little. Allow to soak for a few hours, or overnight if possible. If you don't have a pickle press, put the vegetables in a bowl and weigh them down by resting a plate on top of them.

★ In the meantime, crush the ginger and garlic. Soak the dulse seaweed in cold water for 30 minutes, drain and finely chop.

★ Drain the soaked vegetables, but be sure to keep the brine. Mix the turmeric in with the vegetables, seaweed, crushed ginger and garlic and add the chilli/chile.

★ Put this mixture back into the pickle press or bowl and add enough brine to rise over the veggies once you press them down. Screw the lid down as much as you can, or, if using a plate, put something heavy on top of it. Allow to ferment for a minimum of a week. The best taste develops after 4 weeks.

CREOLE RUB

½ small onion, finely chopped

1 garlic clove, finely chopped

1 tablespoon freshly chopped thyme leaves

1 tablespoon paprika

1 teaspoon ground cumin

1 teaspoon salt

¼ teaspoon cayenne pepper

1 tablespoon soft brown sugar

a pinch of freshly ground black pepper

makes about 6 tablespoons

★ Put all the ingredients in a small bowl, mix well and set aside to infuse until ready to use.

MOROCCAN RUB

1 tablespoon coriander seeds

1 teaspoon cumin seeds

2 cinnamon sticks

1 teaspoon whole allspice berries

6 cloves

a pinch of saffron threads

1 teaspoon ground turmeric

2 teaspoons dried onion flakes

1 teaspoon salt

½ teaspoon paprika

makes about 6 tablespoons

★ Put the whole spices and saffron threads in a dry frying pan/skillet and toast over medium heat for about 1–2 minutes or until golden and aromatic. Remove from the heat and let cool. Transfer to a spice grinder and crush to a coarse powder. Alternatively, use a mortar and pestle.

★ Put the spices in a bowl, add the remaining ingredients and mix well. Set aside to infuse until you are ready to use.

FRAGRANT ASIAN RUB

4 whole star anise

2 teaspoons Szechuan peppercorns

1 teaspoon fennel seeds

2 small pieces of cassia bark or 1 cinnamon stick, broken

6 cloves

2 garlic cloves, finely chopped

grated zest of 2 limes

1 teaspoon salt

makes about 6 tablespoons

★ Put the whole spices in a dry frying pan/skillet and toast over medium heat for 1–2 minutes or until golden and aromatic. Remove from the heat and let cool. Transfer to a spice grinder and crush to a coarse powder. Alternatively, use a mortar and pestle.

★ Put the spices in a bowl, add the garlic, lime zest and salt and mix well. Set aside to infuse until you are ready to use.

CARAMELIZED PINEAPPLE

BRING TROPICAL VIBES TO ANY BARBECUE PARTY WITH FRESHLY GRILLED CARAMELIZED PINEAPPLE. THIS REALLY IS A DELICIOUS DESSERT, REMINISCENT OF SUNSHINE HOLIDAYS BY THE SEA.

1 tablespoon liquid glucose, or a pinch of cream of tartar

200 g/1 cup golden caster/granulated sugar

185 ml/¾ cup coconut milk, at room temperature

40 g/¼ cup skinned pistachio nuts, chopped (optional)

1 pineapple

coconut sorbet, to serve (optional)

serves 8–10

★ To make the caramel, put 60 ml/¼ cup water in a heavy-based pan with the glucose and sugar. Stir to help dissolve the sugar, then gently bring to a simmer over medium heat. It is important not to stir the mixture, just swirl the pan occasionally. Heat until the mixture is clear, then turn up the heat slightly and simmer for 10–15 minutes, until it is deep brown (but not burnt). Remove from the heat, then carefully whisk in the coconut milk – it will splutter so take care. The caramel is served warm but can be refrigerated in a glass bottle for up to a month and reheated.

★ If using pistachios, preheat the oven to 180°C (350°F) Gas 4. Scatter the chopped pistachios over a baking sheet and roast for 5 minutes until slightly browned. Transfer to a bowl and leave to cool.

★ Using a sharp knife, cut the top and bottom off the pineapple, then stand it on one end and cut off the peel and the 'eyes' (cut with a sharp knife from either side, making a small V cut following the diagonal line of the eyes). Cut the pineapple into thick slices, then cut out the central core. Gently reheat the caramel sauce in a small pan over a medium-low heat until warm, if prepared in advance.

★ Preheat the barbecue/grill. Quickly sizzle the pineapple over high heat for 5–7 minutes on each side, until lightly golden. Place on serving plates, drizzle with caramel sauce and scatter over the toasted pistachios. Serve with coconut sorbet, if desired.

SOZZLED APRICOT BRUSCHETTA
with orange cream

THIS IS A SHOW STOPPER, IDEAL FOR WARMING UP GUESTS AT A WINTER COOKOUT. GRILLED PANETTONE TOPPED WITH SOZZLED APRICOTS, LAVISHLY DOLLOPED WITH ORANGE CREAM AND A DECADENT DRIZZLE OF HONEY. IT IS THE MOST DELICIOUS DESSERT TO SERVE WHEN APRICOTS ARE IN SEASON. IF THERE ARE ANY LEFTOVER APRICOTS, STORE IN THE FRIDGE AND HAVE WITH CHEESES OR STIR INTO YOGURT.

240 ml/1 cup good Italian dessert wine

1 vanilla pod/bean, split in half

2 teaspoons soft brown sugar

680 g/1½ lb. (about 18) ripe apricots, halved and pitted

6 slices panettone or brioche, about 4 cm/1½ inches thick

honey, to drizzle

orange cream

240 ml/1 cup crème fraîche or single/light cream

grated zest of 1 orange

1 tablespoon orange blossom honey

3 tablespoons orange liqueur

serves 6

★ Put the Italian dessert wine, vanilla bean/pod and brown sugar in a non-reactive saucepan set over medium–high heat. Bring to a boil then immediately reduce the heat to a simmer. Cook for 5–6 minutes until the sugar has dissolved.

★ Add the apricot halves to the wine and bring to a boil again. Then reduce the heat to medium–low and simmer for a further 10 minutes. You want the apricots to cook but still hold a little of their shape.

★ Remove the apricots from the pan with a slotted spoon and put in a ceramic bowl. Turn the heat back up to medium–high and simmer for about 5 minutes to reduce the poaching liquid by half, stirring frequently. Pour the syrup over the apricots.

★ Preheat the barbecue/grill. While the grill is heating, whisk together the ingredients for the orange cream in a glass bowl and chill in the refrigerator until ready to use.

★ Grill the panettone or brioche slices for about 2 minutes per side, until toasted. Place each one on a plate and spoon the sozzled apricots, along with the juices, over each slice of toasted panettone. Dollop with the orange cream, drizzle with honey and serve.

GRILLED FIGS

with almond mascarpone cream

- -

FIGS ARE AMAZING GRILLED, BUT THIS DISH WOULD
WORK EQUALLY WELL WITH OTHER STONE FRUITS
SUCH AS PLUMS OR PEACHES. TRY TO GET TOP-
QUALITY FRESH FRUIT FROM THE GREENGROCER.

150 g/5 oz. mascarpone cheese

½ teaspoon vanilla extract

1 tablespoon toasted ground
almonds, or flaked/slivered
almonds crushed to a powder
with a mortar and pestle

1 tablespoon Marsala wine

1 tablespoon honey

1 tablespoon sugar

1 teaspoon ground cardamom

8–10 figs, cut in half

serves 4

★ Put the mascarpone cheese, vanilla, almonds, Marsala and honey in a
bowl and beat well. Cover and set aside in the refrigerator until needed.

★ Mix the sugar and ground cardamom in a separate bowl, then carefully
dip the cut surface of the figs in the mixture.

★ Preheat the barbecue/grill.

★ Cook the figs on the hot barbecue/grill for 1–2 minutes on each side
until charred and softened. Transfer the cooked figs to 4 serving bowls
and serve with the almond mascarpone cream.

GRILLED FRUIT PACKAGES

4 peaches or nectarines, cut in half, pitted and sliced

225 g/1½ cups blueberries

15 g/¾ cup raspberries

freshly squeezed juice of 1 orange

1 teaspoon ground cinnamon

2 tablespoons sugar

200 ml/1 cup plain yogurt

2 tablespoons double/heavy cream

1 tablespoon honey

1 tablespoon rose water

1 tablespoon chopped pistachio nuts, to serve

serves 4

WRAPPING FRUITS IN KITCHEN FOIL IS A GREAT WAY TO COOK THEM ON THE BARBECUE/GRILL – ALL THE JUICES AND FLAVOURINGS ARE CONTAINED IN THE PACKAGE WHILE THE FRUIT SOFTENS.

★ Put the fruit in a large bowl, add the orange juice, cinnamon and sugar, and mix well. Divide the fruit mixture evenly between 4 sheets of kitchen foil. Fold the foil over the fruit and seal the edges tightly to make small packages.

★ Mix the yogurt, cream, honey and rose water in a separate bowl. Set aside until needed.

★ Preheat the barbecue/grill.

★ Cook the packages for 5–6 minutes on the hot barbecue/grill. Remove the packages from the heat, open carefully and transfer to 4 serving bowls. Serve with the yogurt and a sprinkling of chopped pistachio nuts.

GRILLED PEARS with spiced honey, walnuts & blue cheese

WHAT A CLASSY WAY TO END A MEAL – THE CLASSIC COMBINATION OF PEARS, BLUE CHEESE AND WALNUTS PERFECTLY COMPLEMENT EACH OTHER, WITH THE ADDED TWIST OF THE SMOKY BARBECUE FLAVOUR. SERVE ON TOAST WITH A GLASS OR TWO OF DESSERT WINE. FOR THE BEST RESULTS, CHOOSE RIPE BUT FIRM PEARS.

50 g/2 oz. walnuts

2 tablespoons honey

¼ teaspoon ground cardamom

4 pears

2 tablespoons caster/
granulated sugar

125 g/4 oz. blue cheese such as
Dolcelatte, Stilton or Danish blue

to serve

toast

dessert wine

wax paper

serves 4

★ Put the walnuts in a frying pan/skillet, add the honey and cardamom, and cook over high heat until the honey bubbles furiously and starts to darken. Immediately pour the mixture onto a sheet of wax paper and let cool.

★ Peel the nuts from the paper and set aside.

★ Preheat the barbecue/grill.

★ Using a sharp knife, cut the pears into quarters and remove and discard the cores. Cut the pear quarters into thick wedges. Dust lightly with sugar and cook on the hot barbecue/grill for 1½ minutes on each side until lightly charred.

★ Pile the pears onto slices of toast, sprinkle with the walnuts and serve with some crumbled blue cheese and a glass of dessert wine.

BAKED BANANA SPLITS
with peanut butter & chocolate

----

cooking oil spray

6 ripe bananas, unpeeled

6 tablespoons crunchy peanut butter

50 g/1¾ oz. Swiss milk chocolate chunks

50 g/1¾ oz. dark/bittersweet chocolate chunks (70% cocoa solids)

6 teaspoons freshly grated or desiccated/shredded coconut (optional)

300 ml/1¼ cups double/heavy cream, whipped

serves 6

WHEN WAS THE LAST TIME YOU HAD A BANANA SPLIT? REMEMBER THE DAYS WHEN SPLITS WERE STUFFED WITH ALL SORTS OF CRAZY ACCOMPANIMENTS, SUCH AS GLACÉ/CANDIED CHERRIES, SUGAR SPRINKLES, SWEET WHIPPED CREAM – AND WHAT ABOUT THE SPARKLERS!? THERE IS SOMETHING HUGELY NOSTALGIC ABOUT THIS UNDERRATED KITSCH DESSERT. THIS RECIPE TAKES FOUR SWEET INGREDIENTS THAT WORK BEAUTIFULLY TOGETHER – CHOCOLATE, PEANUT BUTTER, BANANA AND CREAM. BANANA SPLITS NEVER TASTED SO GOOD!

★ Spray 6 squares of kitchen foil with oil.

★ Using a sharp knife, cut along the inner curve of each banana, about halfway through (enough to open the fruit rather like a book). Spoon a tablespoon of peanut butter into the crack of each banana and spread evenly before filling with chunks of milk and dark chocolate. Sprinkle a teaspoon of coconut over the top of each one, if using, then wrap each banana in its own sheet of foil.

★ Preheat the barbecue/grill.

★ When you are ready to cook, place the bananas directly into the hot embers of the barbecue/grill and leave to cook for about 7–10 minutes. Remove from the heat and carefully unwrap the foil to check if the chocolate is melted and oozing. If so, serve with a dollop of thick cream on the side, otherwise return to the heat and cook for a little longer until the chocolate is molten.

VEGAN MARSHMALLOWS

THERE IS NO NEED TO USE ANIMAL PRODUCTS TO MAKE THE PERFECT MARSHMALLOW. YOU CAN USE GUAR GUM, SOYA/SOY PROTEIN ISOLATE AND A VEGETARIAN GELATINE TO CREATE DELICIOUS VEGAN MARSHMALLOWS. TOAST OVER THE BARBECUE/GRILL WITH COOKIES AND MELTED CHOCOLATE TO SERVE AS DREAMY S'MORES.

180 g/1½ cups icing/confectioners' sugar, plus an extra 30 g/¼ cup for dusting

60 g/½ cup cornflour/cornstarch

light vegetable oil, for greasing

5 tablespoons soya/soy protein isolate 90%

2 teaspoons baking powder

¼ teaspoon guar gum

310 ml/1¼ cups cold water

1 tablespoon Vege Gel, Genutine Vegetarian Gelatine or similar

310 g/1½ cups unrefined/raw sugar

340 g/1 cup golden syrup/light corn syrup

2 teaspoons vanilla extract

cookies and milk chocolate squares for making s'mores (optional)

a jam/candy thermometer

makes 30–35 2.5-cm/1-inch cubed marshmallows

★ In a large bowl, sift 180 g/1½ cups of the icing/confectioners' sugar together with the cornflour/cornstarch and set aside.

★ Oil the bottom and sides of a baking pan, wiping down the pan with paper towels to remove any excess oil. Sift the bottom and sides of the baking pan liberally with the icing/confectioners' sugar and cornflour/cornstarch mixture.

★ Mix the soya/soy protein, baking powder and guar gum together in a stand mixer. Add 180 ml/¾ cup cold water and beat on high for 10 minutes until stiff peaks form. Set aside.

★ Mix the gelatine and unrefined/raw sugar in a large saucepan. Add the remaining water and whisk until thick. Stir in the golden syrup/light corn syrup. Set the saucepan on the stovetop over low heat. Cook the mixture until it reaches 110°C/230°F on a jam/candy thermometer, stirring occasionally. Remove the pan from the heat and quickly stir in the vanilla extract.

★ Slowly add the hot syrup to the soya/soy protein mixture with the stand mixer set on high. Beat the mixture on high for 10 minutes.

★ Pour the mixture into the greased and sugared pan, working as quickly as possible. Sift the remaining icing/confectioners' sugar evenly over the top and let the marshmallows set in the refrigerator for at least 1 hour until firm.

★ Preheat the barbecue/grill. Cut the marshmallow into cubes and toast one over an open flame until it browns and softens. Sandwich a piece of chocolate and the hot marshmallow between two cookies. Let cool slightly before eating.

CHOCOLATE MARSHMALLOW BROWNIES

THESE IRRESISTIBLE BROWNIES ARE BEST ENJOYED WHILE STILL WARM IF YOU WANT TO FULLY EXPERIENCE THE MARSHMALLOWS MELTING INTO THE GOOEY RICH BROWNIES. USE THE VEGAN RECIPE FROM PAGE 139, OR USE STORE-BOUGHT VEGETARIAN MALLOWS IF YOU CAN FIND THEM.

112 g/½ cup butter

50 g/2 oz. dark/bittersweet chocolate (minimum 75% cocoa solids), broken into squares

200 g/1 cup caster/granulated sugar

2 eggs

1 teaspoon vanilla extract

60 g/½ cup plain/all-purpose flour

¼ teaspoon fine salt

1 teaspoon baking powder

25 g/1 oz. Vegan Marshmallows (see page 139), cut into 1-cm/½-inch pieces

a 20-cm/8-inch square brownie pan (or similar), greased and floured

makes about 20 brownies

★ Preheat the oven to 180°C (350°F) Gas 4.

★ Melt the butter and the chocolate together in a heatproof bowl set over a saucepan of barely simmering water. (Make sure the base of the bowl does not touch the water.) Stir occasionally until smooth and combined. Remove from the heat and let cool slightly. Stir in the sugar, eggs and vanilla extract. Beat in the flour, salt and baking powder, taking care not to overmix.

★ Spread half of the batter into the prepared brownie pan. Add three quarters of the marshmallows. Pour the other half of the brownie mixture over the chopped marshmallows and top with the rest of the marshmallows.

★ Bake in the preheated oven for 25–30 minutes, or until slightly springy in the middle. Leave to cool in the pan before removing and cutting into squares to serve.

INDEX

RECIPE CREDITS

Amy Ruth Finegold
Quinoa burgers with portobello mushroom 'buns'

Annie Rigg
Chargrilled halloumi with mixed olive tapenade

Brian Glover
Courgette/zucchini & feta salad with lemon, caper & mint dressing

Carol Hilker
Chocolate marshmallow brownies
Rosemary coleslaw
Vegan marshmallows

Celia Brooks Brown
Thai-glazed vegetable skewers

Chloe Coker and Jane Montgomery
Beet, celeriac/celery root & apple remoulade
Chicory/endive leaves stuffed with beet, cumin & mixed grains
Spinach & ricotta stuffed onions

Claire McDonald and Lucy Mcdonald
Halloumi pitta pockets

Dunja Gulin
Home-fermented kimchi
Spicy vegan burgers

Fran Warde
Grilled courgettes/zucchini

Ghillie Basan
Aubergine/eggplant with honey & spices
Bulgur with ghee
Buttery couscous
Cauliflower fritter satay with coriander/cilantro chutney
Fried carrot & fennel with cumin & pomegranate molasses
Middle Eastern roasted vegetables with pomegranate seeds
Rice pilaf
Roasted pumpkin wedges with lime & spices
Simple noodles with ginger & chilli/chile
Spicy tofu satay with soy dipping sauce
Summer vegetable kebabs with pesto
Tumeric potatoes with lime & coriander/cilantro

Jackie Kearney
Caramelized pineapple
Mango & lime vegetable slaw
Shashlik skewers
Sticky BBQ tofu skewers

Jane Noraika
Aubergine/eggplant & cheese rolls
Plantain with lime & chilli/chile

Jordan Bourke
Aubergine/eggplant gratin
Baba ghanoush
Beet burgers with wholegrain mustard mayonnaise
Borlotti bean purée
Carrot, blood orange & walnut salad
Quinoa salad with spring vegetables
Sweet potato hummus

Laura Washburn
BBQ bread loaf
Mac 'n' cheese with spinach
Mushroom barley burgers
Ratatouille

Lesley Waters
New potato salad with gazpacho dressing

Lindy Wildsmith
Sesame sweet potato packets

Louise Pickford
Asian barbecue sauce
Beet & baby onion brochettes
Blue cheese dressing
Charred leeks with tarator sauce
Chunky aubergine/eggplant burgers
Creole rub
Curried sweet potato burgers
Ember-roasted potatoes
Fragrant Asian rub
Garlic bread skewers
Grilled artichokes with chilli/chile lime mayonnaise
Grilled corn with chilli/chile-salt rub
Grilled figs with almond mascarpone cream
Grilled fruit packages
Grilled pitta salad with olive salsa & mozzarella
Grilled polenta
Grilled rosemary flatbread
Grilled pears with spiced honey, walnuts & blue cheese
Herb, lemon & garlic marinade
Mango & sesame salsa
Minted yogurt marinade
Moroccan rub
Mushroom burgers with chilli/chile mayonnaise & red onion jam
Open tofu bean burgers
Roasted red bell pepper & asparagus salad
Salsa verde
Smoky tomato salsa
Spiced falafel burgers
Sweet chilli/chile sauce
Thai spiced marinade
Vegetable antipasto

Lydia France
Piri piri mushrooms

Miranda Ballard
Cheesy root vegetable burgers
Classic coleslaw
Classic homecut fries
Classic mayo
Herb mayo
Homemade tomato ketchup
Hot & smoky barbecue sauce
Lemon mayo
Mustard mayo
Pesto mayo
Sour cream slaw
Sweet potato wedges

Tori Finch
Baked banana splits with peanut butter & chocolate
Basil, mozzarella & orzo salad
Cornbread muffins with mango guacamole
Grilled vegetable burgers with halloumi 'buns'
Lemon, garlic & chilli/chile potato salad
Pomegranate & squash salad with a balsamic dressing
Salad of soy, wheat berries & cashews
Salad of truffled French beans
Tabbouleh salad with feta

Tori Haschka
Tomato keftedes with tzatziki

Valerie Aikman-Smith
Grilled market vegetable salad with herbed toasts
Sozzled apricot bruschetta with orange cream

PICTURE CREDITS